Congressman Philip Crane

"I only wish that those responsible for the Treaties had had the chance to read this book in 1977. It might very well have changed the disastrous course of events."

Philip M. Crane, Member of Congress, comments on Captain G. Russell Evans' first book, Panama Canal Treaties Swindle: Consent to Disaster

Senator Jesse Helms

In organizing the petition effort, the National Security Center made a valuable contribution in our efforts to prevent President Clinton from sending this controversial nominee to Panama. I personally and genuinely appreciate the National Security Center's help in making known the (Robert) Pastor record.

Jesse Helms, U.S. Senator, comments on work of the publisher, National Security Center

Admiral Thomas H. Moorer

This book should be must reading for every citizen concerned with the security, prosperity, and world image of the United States. It relates in detail just how the Panama Canal Treaties came into being and what impact these unconstitutional Treaties have had and will have on the future of our country. There's plenty here the public should know about, particularly after the incursion into Panama by that budding maritime superpower, Communist China, as is detailed in this book.

I am astounded when I hear supposedly intelligent officers and officials state that the Canal no longer has any strategic value.

Admiral Thomas H. Moorer, former chairman of the Joint Chiefs of Staff, from the Introduction

Richard A. Delgaudio

Captain G. Russell Evans—together with Senator Jesse Helms and Congressman Philip Crane—has been a prophet warning about the dire consequences to U.S. economic and security interests if the giveaway of U.S. property at the Panama Canal goes through as planned. This book demolishes every argument put forward by the appeasers and gives the lie to arm-chair conservative and GOP "leaders" who take the donations of grassroots conservatives but do little or nothing to change the policy of the ruling elites of Panama and the United States—policies which are indeed sounding the "death knell" of that eighth wonder of the world, the American-built Panama Canal.

Richard A. Delgaudio, President, National Security Center, publisher of Death Knell of the Panama Canal?

Death Knell

of the

Panama Canal?

**The fate of the 8th Wonder of the World since the United States relinquished control
to the Panama Canal Commission
(ABRIDGED)**

Captain G. Russell Evans
USCG (Ret.)

Foreword by
Richard A. Delgaudio, President
National Security Center

Introduction by
Admiral Thomas H. Moorer, U.S. Navy (Ret.)
Former Chairman of the Joint Chiefs of Staff

ON THE COVER

This striking aerial photo shows the 3-step Gatun Locks on the Atlantic side of the Canal, looking South into Gatun Lake, the largest man-made lake in the world at the time of its creation 1908-1914. Gatun Locks, double-chambered, lifts South-bound ships 85 feet into Gatun Lake and lower North-bound ships 85 feet into the Caribbean Sea. These Locks are flanked by earthen dams, largest in the world when constructed in 1910-1912. (Photo/Panama Canal Commission.)

In honor of Russ, Jr. and Sam

Sons to be proud of

Published by

National Security Center
Freedom Center
10560 Main St. #217
Fairfax, Virginia 22030

ISBN: 0-9658348-0-8

First Press Run, Spring 1998
Second Press Run, Fall 1998
Third Pass Run, Spring 1999

ACKNOWLEDGMENTS

First, we acknowledge and thank the thousands and thousands of supporters of the National Security Center (NSC) for their financial contributions that make NSC possible, including three important fact-finding missions to Panama—and for their encouraging and enthusiastic letters, notes and telephone calls that let us know how much they care. All organizations need staff people and shelter and food, and NSC supporters understand this.

Next, special thanks to Richard A. Delgaudio, President of the National Security Center, for his vision and steadfast dedication to our goal of saving the Canal and strategic U.S. bases in Panama—and for his foresight and courage in publishing this book to update the scandalous developments cascading upon us in surrendering this Wonder of the World and Pride of America: The Panama Canal.

Thanks also to Richard's associates, David Tyson and Dan Lewis, who labor in mysterious silence in developing ideas and scenarios for NSC adventures—even book publishing! All good.

The NSC Board of Directors, under Chairman Donald A. Derham, Director Mike Zummo and others provide direction and judgment.

The day-to-day working staff at NSC are acknowledged with much appreciation, especially James Hogan, Managing Editor of the PANAMA ALERT newsletter and that jewel Susan Kutyba, Administrative Assistant, who turned out a gorgeous product with her computer—something only computer experts know how to do! This lady's work on the book manuscript was phenomenal.

Now to the power panel of our National Security

team: First is Admiral Thomas H. Moorer, U.S. Navy (Ret.) and former Chairman of the Joint Chiefs of Staff, who provided the outstanding Introduction and has been a source of expertise and judgment. He is also the senior member of NSC's Retired Military Officers Advisory Board.

Our appreciation also goes to the 22 other military officers who have indicated their support of NSC projects by their service on the Military Advisory Board.

We acknowledge with special thanks the information provided by Bill Bright Marine, dual citizen of Panama and the United States and who is an announced candidate for President of Panama in the 1999 elections.

For the excellent photos of the Canal and environs, we are indebted to Willie K. Friar, Director of Public Affairs of the Panama Canal Commission and her staff, always very cooperative in publicizing the Canal.

We are very appreciative of the assistance, during our 1995 Mission to Panama, provided by Captain Ralph Mendenhall, retired senior Panama Canal Pilot; Ray Bishop, veteran labor leader of Panama; and Luis Rivera for his expert driving and contacts around Panama City. Bishop and Rivera were very valuable in arranging interviews.

Now, some very special thanks to Anne—my wife and collaborator in all my projects—also, "Nurse of the Year" in helping me back to health after 6-way bypass heart surgery. Her inspiration and approval are important ingredients!

It is a pleasure to acknowledge and thank the following additional individuals for the valuable information provided in interviews, letters and telephone discussions during the period 1987-1997, the period covered by this book:

Dr. Donald A. Alberts, Sr., economist and President

of All Points Association, Inc.; Nancy Agris, legislative aide to Chairman George W. Crockett, D-Mich., Chairman of the House Committee on Western Hemisphere Affairs; Elliott Abrams, Assistant Secretary of State for Inter-American Affairs; Ben Baldwin, radio talk show host for station WOAI of San Antonio, Texas.

Panamanian President Ernesto "Toro" Perez Balladares; Raymond Balland, Panama Desk, State Department; Rep. Dan Burton, R-Ind., Chairman House Committee on Western Hemisphere Affairs; Brig. Gen. Richard E. Brown III, Commander 24th Air Wing, U.S. Air Force, Panama; Elizabeth Bollman, economic counselor, U.S. Embassy, Panama; Olegario Balleller, Vice President, Chase Manhattan Bank, Panama; Larry Birns, Director, Council on Hemispheric Affairs; Senator Robert C. Beverly, California State Senate.

Rep. Philip M. Crane, R-Ill.; Martin Coleman, political analyst; Rear Admiral David L. Chandler, Deputy Commander-in-Chief, U.S. Southern Command; Juan Correa, General Manager, La Prensa; Mayin Correa P., Mayor of Panama City; Dr. Ruben Carles, Panamanian presidential candidate 1994; Senator William A. Craven, California State Senate; Rep. George W. Crockett, D-Mich., Chairman of House Committee on Western Hemisphere Affairs.

Dr. Donald L. Donohugh of Kauai, Hawaii, NSC member; Tom DeWeese, President of American Policy Center; Panamanian President Guillermo Endara; Roberto Eisenmann, Jr., publisher La Prensa; Fernando Eleta, former Panamanian Foreign Minister; Roger Fontaine, political analyst; Hugo Famania, host TV show "Breakfast in Panama"; Alonzo Fernandez, former President Panamanian National Assembly; James Ferrara, Director, Canal Transition Commission; Panamanian Vice President Guillermo "Billy" Ford; Victoria Figge, President, Panama Association of Professional Businessmen; Rep. Dante B. Fascell, D-Fla.

Gabriel Lewis Galindo, Panamanian Foreign Minister; Rep. Benjamin A. Gilman, R-N.Y.; Gilberto Guardia F., Panama Canal Administrator; Oliver Garcia, Charge d'Affaires, U.S. Embassy, Panama; Senator Jesse Helms, R-N.C., Chairman, Foreign Relations Committee; Peter Hakim, President, InterAmerican Dialogue Group; Richard Kosler, author of In Time of Tyrants; Mike Kozak, legal adviser to the Secretary of State in 1978; Rep. Peter Kostmeyer, D-Pa.

Commander Horace M. Leavitt III, U.S. Navy, staff of the Joint Chiefs of Staff; Raymond P. Laverty, Deputy Administrator of the Panama Canal; Panamanian President Demetrio B. Lakas (1970-1979); Rep. Robert J. Lagomarsino, R-Cal.; Fernando Manfredo, Acting Administrator of the Panama Canal; Dr. Carlos Mendoza, President of the Interceanic Region Authority, Panama; John Mohanco, labor counselor, U.S. Embassy in Panama; Dr. Richard Millett, Director, North-South Center; Dr. Robert Morris, Chairman of America's Future.

David Noble, Panama Desk, State Department; Lt. Colonel Richard Nazario, U.S. Army, Treaties Implementation, U.S. Southern Command, Panama; Major Joseph C. Myers, U.S. Army, Treaties Implementation, U.S. Southern Command, Panama; Charles Orndorff, Administrative Chairman, The Conservative Caucus; Lt. Colonel Arne Owens, U.S. Army, Department of Defense representative on Panama Canal Treaties; Maria Cristina Ozores T., owner and publisher of La Estrella de Panama; Victor A. Ortiz, Director, Panama Chamber of Commerce; Colonel Richard O'Connor, Director, Treaties Implementation, U.S. Southern Command, Panama.

Howard Phillips, Chairman, The Conservative Caucus; General Colin Powell, U.S. Army, Chairman, Joint Chiefs of Staff; Carolyn Piper, staff member, Joint Chiefs of Staff; Rep. Owen Pickett, D-Va.; Anne Patterson, Deputy Assistant Secretary of State for InterAmerican Affairs; Benin Pasqual, civil engineer member of Panama Association of Professional Businessmen; U.S. Vice President Dan Quayle; Captain Arthur N. Rowley III, U.S. Navy, Commanding Officer, Rodman Naval Station; Mike Rotolo, President, Combined Chambers of Commerce, Panama; Senator Don Rogers, California State Senate; Senator David Roberto, California State Senate; Dr. Charles E. Rice, Notre Dame Law School.

Maj. General John K. Singlaub, U.S. Army; Frederick C. Smith, Deputy Assistant Secretary of Defense for International Affairs; Colonel Ray Smith, U.S. Army (Ret.); Rep. Stephen Solares, D-N.Y.; Donna Thiessen, legislative aide to Rep. Philip M. Crane, R-Ill.; Paul A. Trivilli, State Department, Director, Central American Affairs; Raymond B. Underwood, President, Levonel, Inc., Panama; Gary S. Usrey, Counsul General, Panama.

Joaquin J. Vallarino, Chairman, President's Commission on the Panama Canal, Panama; Jose Ramon Varela C., Secretary, Panama Chamber of Commerce; Carol van Voost, political counselor, U.S. Embassy, Panama; Eduardo Vallarino, Panamanian presidential candidate 1994; Steve Weste, political officer, U.S. Embassy, Panama.

Norfolk, Va.
May 31, 1997

G. Russell Evans
Chief Adviser, Panama Canal
National Security Center

FOREWORD

In 1976 as a fieldman for Reagan for President, I recall being told by some conservatives that only a couple of congressmen had endorsed Ronald Reagan for President and so he had no chance. And, I was also told, nobody would understand what he was talking about when he said the U.S. should stand up for its interests at the Panama Canal. After all, how many Americans even knew where this Canal was, let alone why it might be important to America?

As it turned out, Ronald Reagan came to within 100 delegate votes of winning the presidential nomination from a sitting President of his own party, and won rather convincingly four years later.

And as it turned out, the Panama Canal issue was used by a number of U.S. Senate candidates who ran with Ronald Reagan on this issue and who took control of the U.S. Senate from those who voted for Jimmy Carter's appeasement treaties.

Today, with another appeaser in the White House, America's interests are not being safeguarded at the Panama Canal. In fact, America's interests may have been sold to Red China by the current occupant of that office, something that Congress should look into.

The National Security Center is proud to have worked with Captain G. Russell Evans to report on the continuing importance of the Panama Canal to America's economic and security interests.

This has been an emotional issue in the past, in fact, it has been called a "bumper-sticker" issue. Many otherwise reasonable conservatives have shied away from this issue because of the fear that they might be perceived as "pandering" on an emotional issue.

Yet as Ronald Reagan demonstrated, this is an important issue, the American people are concerned about it. And as we have learned more recently and as is documented in this book, concerned Panamanian citizens have the same concerns that we Americans do— and by the same 75-80% margins. The economic and security interests of the citizens of both countries are tied to an effectively run and secure Panama Canal. Only a continued U.S. military presence at the bases and the ports of the Panama Canal can promise a sound future for all concerned. We are proud to publish this book to help document the case.

This publication, and indeed all of our work, is made possible by the generous financial support of many donors to the National Security Center. Most of our supporters send an average of $15. A few send a much larger $1000, and many are in between. To all of them, we say "thank you—you are the wind beneath our wings."

Richard A. Delgaudio
President
National Security Center

Death Knell of the Panama Canal?

National Security Center
Retired Military Officers Advisory Board

CONTENTS (Abridged Version)

PREFACE

We selected the title, Death Knell of the Panama Canal?—with a question mark—in order to highlight the dangers that could result from startling developments at the Isthmus of Panama, as the date for surrender of the Canal approaches: December 31, 1999.

Some things are wrong at the Panama Canal—wrongs that could doom this great waterway and world-famous monument to American engineering genius and generosity—all because of a timid U.S. president who valued appeasement and international popularity above his own country's rights and security: Jimmy Carter.

As the surrender date approaches, three major developments threaten the future of Canal operations and may be harbingers of the death knell of what Admiral Tom Moorer, former Chairman of the Joint Chiefs of Staff, has called, "the most vital maritime gateway in the entire world":

Something is wrong when the Canal operators, the Panama Canal Commission, allow deterioration of major components of the Canal system because of "lack of maintenance caused by the need to lock ships" for more Canal tolls.

Something is wrong when the Government of Panama, sole operator of the Canal after 1999, on March 1, 1997 turns over the controlling ports of Balboa and Cristobal at each end of the Canal to allies of Communist China, who calls the United States "our main enemy," and awards them a 50-year lease, expanding "rights" that infringe on U.S. rights under the 1977 Panama Canal Treaties.

Something is wrong when the Government of the United States continues to accept unconstitutional

Treaties and condones Red Chinese incursions at the strategic Panama Canal against Treaty rights.

This 83-year old treasure at the "most strategic chokepoint in the world"—so vital to the security and economy of the United States and Panama—is "wearing out... due to lack of maintenance," quoting from the 1996 Operations and Maintenance Study by the U.S. Army Corps of Engineers, called "politically sensitive" by the Canal operators, the Panama Canal Commission, who initiated the study.

This Army report discloses crumbling concrete and corroding infrastructure, along with a lack of "commitment to see that proper maintenance is done." Some features, however, are called "good." Obviously, the desire for more tolls and more traffic delayed maintenance, as the Canal moved increasingly toward Panamanian control. More ships mean more tolls, and more tolls mean a fatter national treasury for Panama after the 1999 takeover.

As for a fat Panamanian treasury, let us note the 1996 "Panama Canal Declaration," drawn up by political elitists and endorsed by former President Guillermo Endara. This "Declaration" is concerned with short-term gains—for example, deposit of the "largest percentage possible" of Canal tolls in the national treasury. This means no more nonprofit Canal operations, as under the United States, plus increased potential for corruption and embezzlement of funds and increased tolls that eventually will drive shipping companies to seek more economical routes.

Unconstitutional Treaties and the deteriorating Canal are enough to bring on the death knell of this great waterway, but the surprise incursions of the Communist Chinese can virtually guarantee the death knell of the Canal, as Americans know it.

Panama wants big bucks for everything about the Canal and its environs—and apparently Treaty rights and security of the Canal mean nothing. Consequently, its Legislative Assembly passed Law No. 5 on January 16, 1997 giving control of the strategic ports of Balboa and Cristobal to Hutchison Whampoa of Hong Kong, a close ally of Communist China, which, on July 1, 1997, took over Hong Kong and domination, control and direction of Hutchison. Thus, Hutchison works for Red China.

Panama's Law No. 5 was a secretive deal, receiving virtually no publicity until it was a done-deal. Among other things, this Law violates Article 274 of Panama's Constitution that requires a plebiscite on Canal matters. None was held. It also violates Article VI of the Panama Canal Neutrality Treaty by, in effect, denying "expeditious treatment" of U.S. warships needing port facilities at the Canal.

How did Panama pull this off? Simple! At first, the bidding on the ports was open to all comers. Then, President Balladares closed the bidding, changed the rules and awarded the $22.2 million per year contract to Hutchison, the Red Chinese ally—all before the American bidders knew what happened.

What did happen? Panamanian newspapers reported "bucket loads of money" pouring in from Asian contractors and "money under the table" from the Chinese—obviously, standard operating procedure for the Chinese. At this time, in the fall of 1996, Red Chinese money was pouring into President Clinton's campaign coffers, according to media reports. The Clinton Administration said nothing, before or after the Chinese incursions into Panama. Was this a quid pro quo?

Money talks! Big money talks big—and political money moves mountains. In the case of the Canal, political money could be the difference between a secure Canal and its death knell.

This book, Death Knell of the Panama Canal?, is a sequel to our first book about Panama, The Panama Canal Treaties Swindle: Consent to Disaster (Signal Books). The sub-title of this first book, Consent to Disaster, seems prophetic as, ten years later, the Communists move in as the Americans move out, leaving a deteriorated Canal, invading Communists and a greedy Panamanian regime to run the show.

This book title might well have been Swindle of the Century. Indeed, who can recall a bigger fraud in the 20th century, or any other century, than the deprivation of 32 billion dollars worth of U.S. taxpayers property, territory and rights under false pretenses—false pretenses, the most insulting way to steal—all done by a neophyte president out to do good and make a name for himself as an international philanthropist?

If this scandalous swindle is consummated, Americans will have surrendered the greatest single achievement of our 221 year history, the most meaningful contribution ever made by one nation for the benefit of all nations, and most important, we may have "written the final chapter in the history of America's greatness as a world power," quoting James Farrell in The Judas Syndrome (Fulton-Hall), page 15—and it will all have been done by deliberate violations of the Constitution of the United States.

In future years, because of these fraudulent Treaties, America will have no choice but to use force to claim its legitimate rights. Then, the charges by Panama of the "misdeeds" of Teddy Roosevelt in the original 1903 Treaty and Frenchman Bunau-Varilla, Treaty negotiator, will be dwarfed by denouncements of the Carter-Torrijos swindle.

This, along with deterioration of the Canal from neglected maintenance, the incursions of the Communist Chinese with far-reaching "rights" that may eventually control this chokepoint and the failure to welcome the United States as a partner in operating the Canal can eventually cause the death knell that could reverberate around the world.

The best arrangement for the Panama Canal, as the surrender date of December 31, 1999 approaches, is a U.S.-Panama partnership—best for Panama, best for the United States and best for world commerce.

Norfolk, Va.   G. Russell Evans
May 31, 1997   Chief Adviser, Panama Canal
                   National Security Center

INTRODUCTION

This book should be must reading for every citizen concerned with the security, prosperity, and world image of the United States. It relates in detail just how the Panama Canal Treaties came into being and what impact these unconstitutional Treaties have had and will have on the future of our country. There's plenty here the public should know about, particularly the incursion into Panama by that budding maritime superpower, Communist China, as is detailed in this book.

The Treaties were signed by President Carter and Torrijos, the dictator of Panama, and by the terms of these agreements the Canal and all installations will revert to the ownership of the Republic of Panama at noon on 31 December 1999. The clock is ticking. Only two and a half short years are left for possible agreement mutually advantageous for both parties.

Subsequent to the signing in 1977 the United States has turned over to Panama several installations which have been allowed to rapidly deteriorate. And of vital importance, the Canal itself is beginning to show signs of unsatisfactory maintenance. All told about 32 billion dollars worth of equipment and bases paid for by the American taxpayer is changing hands.

I will never understand why President Carter and the Democrats in the Senate were so obsessed with the passing of these Treaties. In his first book, President Carter stated that he was well aware that about two thirds of the American people were opposed to the Treaties and yet he went right ahead. There were far more disadvantages than advantages for the United States contained in the total transfer of the Canal. Even today our national strategy depends heavily on major use of the Canal.

I am astounded when I hear supposedly intelligent officers and officials state that the Canal no longer has any strategic value. The United States is a maritime nation. During this century we have fought all wars overseas.

About 95% of our routine logistic support goes by sea. This invariably demands major transfers from one ocean to the other via the Panama Canal of cargo as well as combat ships. I have had considerable opportunity during several wars to observe the vital importance of the Panama Canal. Under the terms of these Treaties, Panama has no defensive forces. Therefore, if any outside power seized the Canal or attempted to close it, the United States would be forced to retake it immediately in case of war.

I feel very strongly about the importance of the Panama Canal and I testified several times before the Congress opposing this giveaway. The major support for the Canal Treaties in the Congress existed in the Foreign Relations Committee, chaired by Senator Frank Church, who was strongly supported by Senator Paul Sarbanes and Senator Joseph Biden. It seemed to me that their primary motivation was based on emotion rather than reason. Their position was, in effect, that if we give the Canal away, then people will love us; if we don't give it away, people will hate us; and if we don't give it away, Torrijos and his henchmen will destroy it.

They did not appear to be concerned by either the strategic or commercial factors, both of which were significant. Accordingly, when put to a vote, the "Advice and Consent" passed with 68 votes, only one and one third more than required. President Cater then invited Torrijos, the Dictator of Panama, to Washington and amid great fanfare, they both signed the Panama Canal Treaties. When Torrijos overflew Cuba on his way back to Panama, he and Castro had a congratulatory conversation about Torrijos' "victory".

However, at this time, the United States Constitution and Panama's Constitution came into play in connection with the following:

The Reservation proposed by Senator DeConcini was never properly brought up for a vote in Panama. This Reservation was very important. It provided to the United States the right to re-enter Panama if hostile action threatened the continuous operation of the Canal.

When Torrijos was apprised of the DeConcini Reservation, he promptly added counter provisions to the copies of the Treaties that he held, requiring Panama's "cooperation" for United States defense of the Canal.

According to the Panama Constitution, only President Lakas, rather than Torrijos, was authorized to sign the Treaties for Panama.

According to the United States Constitution, the House of Representatives must also vote to dispose of property of the United States. This requirement was not properly complied with before ratifying the Treaties by President Carter.

So clearly, the Panama Canal Treaties are unconstitutional. Furthermore, the Congress was fully aware of this. In the Congressional Record, Serial No. J-98-47, Senator Sarbanes, one of the floor managers for the Treaties in the Senate, is quoted as follows:

"I am now quoting Charles G. Fenwick, International Law: 'Since the signature of a treaty represents the meeting of the minds of the several parties upon specific provisions involving reciprocal obligations, any changes or amendments inserted by one party as a condition of ratification must be accepted by the other party if the treaty is to come into legal effect."'

I am confident that a careful read of this book will convince the reader that the Panama Canal Treaties are illegal and due to the fact that under the terms of the Treaties, all property and facilities will "revert" to Panama in just two and a half years, some kind of partnership of mutual benefit should be worked out as a matter of high priority. I think President Reagan was right when he said:

"We bought it, we paid for it, it's ours, and we are going to keep it".

McLean, Va.   Thomas H. Moorer
May 1, 1997   Admiral, U.S. Navy (Ret.)
                       Former Chairman,
                       Joint Chiefs of Staff

CHAPTER 1

'The Least Intelligent
Strategic Decision'

The unprecedented surrender of $32 billion worth of U.S. taxpayers' property at the Isthmus of Panama, including the Panama Canal—totally against the will of the owners, the American people, and in gross violation of the U.S. Constitution and Panama's Constitution—remains unchallenged as the Swindle of the Century.

These illegal Treaties together with the 1996 U.S. Army Corps of Engineers State-of-the-Canal study that found the Canal "wearing out" from lack of maintenance have become a double-barreled threat to hasten the death knell of this great waterway.

First, an update on the details of the swindle, called "the greatest fraud ever perpetrated against the United States Senate and against the American people."

Indeed, in the history of the world, who can name a fraud more costly, more arrogant and done in a sneakier manner than the 1977 Carter-Torrijos Panama Canal Treaties of 1977?

Renowned Army General John K. Singlaub was canned in 1977 by President Jimmy Carter for telling the truth about the real cost of appeasement on the Korean peninsula—that is, withdrawing too many U.S. troops would invite attack by the Communist North and hence endanger the peace and endanger U.S. soldiers' lives. Later, when Jimmy Carter was saying, "It won't cost the taxpayers a dime," and denigrating those who expressed concerns about his giveaway on strategic grounds, the outspoken Singlaub called the Panama Treaties, "the least intelligent strategic decision since the founding of the Republic"—a polite way of saying they're the dumbest things he'd ever heard of.

'The most substantive change'

President Carter and Panamanian Dictator Omar Torrijos could not get Treaties legally and honestly, so they connived by telephone on April 7, 1978 to sneak in Panama's secret counter-reservation that killed unilateral U.S. defense rights, that Torrijos objected to and that had been guaranteed by the U.S. DeConcini Reservation.

And speaking of sneaky, this Panamanian counter-reservation became "the most substantive change imaginable," was never voted on by the U.S. Senate for "Advice and Consent" and indeed, was never revealed to the public until June 16, 1978 when the State Department handlers passed out press releases after Dictator Torrijos had signed the Instruments of Ratification in Panama City, Panama—too late for Senate objections or public uproar. As a one-time sneak, this one has to be tops!

Appendix A quotes Panama's three-paragraph counter-reservation which, in the second paragraph, requires "mutual respect and cooperation" for any U.S. defense or reopening of the Canal. Obviously, if Panama decided not to "cooperate," the United States could not legally enter to defend or reopen a threatened Canal. Failure of the U.S. Senate to approve this major change was a serious violation of Article II of the U.S. Constitution.

Failure of the Democratic floor manager of the Treaties, Senator Paul S. Sarbanes, D-Md., to alert his colleagues to this counter-reservation constituted a critical breakdown in integrity.

Just how important was Mr. Sarbanes' lapse in integrity? Apparently, it was the single most critical manipulation that allowed the Treaties to pass. A survey in 1982 proved that eight senators would have voted against the Treaties if they had seen this counter-reservation. Therefore, the Treaties would have failed.

False pretenses: Hallmark of a swindle

Why are the Panama Treaties a swindle? Because they would deprive American taxpayers of their property, territory and rights under false pretenses. That's the hallmark of a swindle. The dictionary emphasizes "false pretenses." Surrender of the Canal and its supporting installations will not be a theft or a giveaway, but a swindle.

Many patriotic organizations since the turbulent negotiations of 1977-78 have strongly opposed surrender of this American treasure, the Panama Canal, but, as far as we know, only the National Security Center (NSC) and myself, as NSC chief adviser on the Panama Canal, have emphasized the swindle aspect—the theft of property and rights under false pretenses. False pretenses are the ultimate insult to Americans in this disgraceful episode, about which they had no say-so or control—only frustration.

Meanwhile, dawdling seems to be the order of the day for any "exploratory talks" for base rights negotiations, as agreed by President Clinton and Panamanian President Ernesto "Toro" Perez Balladares at their Oval Office meeting September 6, 1995.

From press reports, it seems that Mr. Balladares is

having second thoughts, as he travels around Europe for better deals in future uses of the American facilities. Appendix B is a column from The Washington Times reporting some of the details.

Principals in the swindle

A few of the principals involved in forcing unconstitutional Treaties on the American people include President Carter, Treaties co-negotiator Sol Linowitz, Secretaries of State Henry Kissinger and Cyrus Vance, President Lyndon Johnson and Senator Howard Baker, R-Tenn.

President Carter deceived the voters in 1976 by promising never to give up control of the Canal. He also promised never to lie to us. He said many times that he wanted "justice for Panama." He broke these promises the first day he was President by signing the order to commence negotiations to surrender the Canal. "Justice for America" was not a consideration. He failed utterly to understand the vital strategic and economic importance of the Canal. What Mr. Carter did do well, however, was to deceive voters about his intentions.

Henry Kissinger, as Secretary of State in 1974, in what was a grandstand play with Panamanian Foreign Minister Juan Tack, signed the infamous Statement of Principles, alleging incorrectly in three of the eight principles that the Canal Zone was Panamanian territory, whereas, the U.S. Supreme Court had ruled in 1907 in Wilson v. Shaw that the Zone was "unincorporated U.S. Territory." Same for the U.S. Court of Appeals for the 5th Circuit in 1972 in U.S. v. Husband R. (Roach).

How could any Secretary of State make such an inexcusable blunder? Or, was it deliberate, a forerunner of the modern hysteria for "political correctness" in the New World Order? This Statement of Principles became the basis for the Panama Canal Treaties of 1977. Henry had given away the store. Little was left to negotiate.

Cyrus Vance, as Secretary of State for Jimmy Carter, supervised the Treaties preparation and shepherding through the Senate. It was certainly his responsibility to see that constitutional procedures were honored. He had sworn his oath to "protect and defend" the Constitution. His responsibility also included controlling his live-wire deputy legal advisor, Mike Kozak, who, it appears, had a great deal to do with handling the Treaties for the State Department.

Sol Linowitz, Treaties negotiator, in trying to sell the Treaties to the public, generated the most boos and guffaws of the season from a combined civic clubs meeting in Houston in 1978 when he alleged that it was "understood, though not in the Treaties, that U.S. warships had head of line privileges." Club members roared in ridicule, but Sol won in the end: The Treaties were "ratified" and the Constitution largely ignored.

Moreover, Mr. Linowitz was interested in collecting the 115 million dollar debt owed by Panama to his bank, the Marine-Midland Bank, of which he was a director—a gross conflict of interest. Later, Linowitz resigned his directorship after exposure by Senator Jesse Helms, R-NC.

Incidentally, Senator Helms was a great fighter to save the Canal, before and after the Treaties, and some of the U.S. bases. His conservative views were often criticized. Appendix C covers one such incident.

As a treaty negotiator, Linowitz had been given a six-months appointment by President Carter in order to avoid Senate confirmation and potential exposure of other embarrassing associations of Linowitz, e.g., registered agent of the communist government of Chile, registered agent of Colombia, next door to Panama and with a real interest in the future of the Canal.

Linowitz had been a long-time advocate of "justice for Panama" in his position as Chairman of the Commission on United States-Latin America Relations—hardly a negotiator to protect American interests.

President Lyndon Johnson was apparently badly frightened after the 1964 Flag Riots in Panama and announced on September 24, 1965 that the basic 1903 Hay-Bunau-Varilla Treaty would be abrogated and that U.S. rights of sovereignty in the Canal Zone would be relinquished.

Thus, Johnson threw away all bargaining chips for negotiations. He assumed authority he did not have and demonstrated pathetic ignorance of constitutional procedures.

Senator Howard Baker, R-Tenn., as Republican Majority Leader in the Senate, decided to support the Treaties, thereby carrying some six Republican senators with him and guaranteeing the two-thirds vote of approval. Mr. Baker provided the margin for victory for Carter.

Diametrically opposite views characterized the Treaties. In many instances, there was never a "meeting of minds," a very necessary ingredient in all treaty-making.

Said Romulo Escobar Bethancourt, chief Panamanian negotiator and fiery Communist agitator, "If the Gringos with their warships say, 'I want to go first,' then, that is their problem. We cannot go that far."

Said Cyrus Vance, U.S. Secretary of State, ". . . our ships can go to the head of the line."

CHAPTER 2

What about Renting the Bases?

In his testimony before the House Subcommittee on the Western Hemisphere in 1995, Congressman Phil Crane, R-Ill., recommended a landlord-tenant arrangement for renting the bases, similar to provisions in other countries. He also recommended certain trade advantages for Panama and a guarantee of U.S. defense of Panama if threatened—all in the spirit of good neighbors.

So, the big question appears to be: Should the United States totally reject the payment of rent? Several flag officers I've talked to say, "No. We pay Spain for the use of Rota; why not Panama?"

Take a deep breath

Perhaps we should take a deep breath and consider the following: (1) Jimmy Carter got us into this mess. (2) The price of liberty and security is not cheap. (3) Maybe we should swallow and negotiate the best deal we can get out of Panama, pressuring them with the proven facts that the Treaties are unconstitutional and definitely a potential for future trouble, with both nations at fault for allowing such embarrassing Treaties. (4) We need those bases and, Jimmy Carter and Sol Linowitz notwithstanding, we should make sure we get them.

On the question of paying rent to Panama, it seems superfluous to the main question of whether U.S. and

Panamanian interests could best be served by a continuation of a U.S. military presence to safeguard the Canal. The question of rent payments should not be allowed to sidetrack the main question.

Update on Phil Crane's resolution

An update on Congressman Phil Crane's resolution, H. Con. Res. 4, is in order. For many years, this patriotic Illinois congressman has faithfully introduced his resolution seeking to abrogate the illegal Panama Treaties outright or, at least, to hold onto several of the superb U.S. installations in Panama. He has traveled to Panama, interviewed many leaders and made many speeches for this cause. Usually, he has had dozens of co-sponsors for his resolution, but never anywhere close to a majority of the House. There have been too many Democrats to support Jimmy Carter's folly and others wanting "justice for Panama" without really understanding the Canal's vital strategic and economic importance to the United States and the mutuality of interests for both nations to have a secure and stable Panama Canal.

CHAPTER 3

What U.S. Officials Told Me

The former Chairman of the Joint Chiefs, General Colin Powell, U.S. Army, told Panamanian President Guillermo Endara in 1994 that "the U.S. was pulling out and would not need any bases after 1999." This apparently caused Endara to change his mind about supporting U.S. base rights. That's what he told me in Panama in 1995 on an NSC hosted Fact Finding Mission to Panama.

I asked General Powell about this and his opinion about continuing some of the bases in a letter. His answer was sketchy, but he did say, "(We) would have no need for all the bases we have maintained...but bases is a matter to be decided between the two governments." Not exactly a direct answer—of course the two governments will decide, but General Powell, what do you think?

Still mystified, I followed up with a query about what specific bases he would favor retaining, e.g., Howard Air Force Base, Rodman Naval Station, Fort Sherman, Galeta Island and Quarry Heights Headquarters for the U.S. Southern Command (SOUTHCOM), but received no answer.

Of course, General Powell does not have to answer me, but it would be nice since he's got the reputation of being a knowledgeable military strategist and scores nicely in public opinion polls for President of the United States. People assume his reputation for knowledge in military affairs translates to a willingness to assert U.S.

strategic and defense interests. Sadly, my personal experience leaves me unconvinced.

I think the American people would welcome General Powell's advice on issues such as the Panama Canal but instead the supposedly Republican General Powell has in common with the leader of the Democratic Party, President Clinton, an aversion to talking about U.S. strategic and security interests at the Panama Canal. Considering Bill Clinton's background, as an anti-war protester, this might not surprise people, but the aversion to speaking out on this vital security interest by General Powell is surprising to me.

President Clinton is asked about bases

In my letter of May 1, 1996, I asked President Clinton to consider the importance of continuing some of the U.S. installations in Panama after 1999, and named the installations. Further, I asked if he would kindly ask Panamanian President Balladares to honor his promise of September 6, 1995 to hold "exploratory talks" on this subject, pointing out that Balladares was now looking to the Europeans for investments and industry developments on the U.S. properties being surrendered to Panama in 1999—apparently with no concern for the future protection and security of the Canal. I felt I'd made a good case.

My answer came back on July 24th via the State Department's Central American Affairs Acting Director Paul A. Trivilli who wrote: (1) Both governments were committed to the process and the American Ambassador and Panamanian officials are continuing an "informal dialogue." (2) Neutrality of the Canal can be fulfilled without a continuing U.S. military presence in Panama, but a post-1999 presence could be in the U.S. interest in counter-narcotics activities, logistical support, training, humanitarian action and search and rescue missions. (3) The United States is not prepared to pay rent for access to bases in Panama.

Defense Department mum on specific bases

I asked the Joint Chiefs representative Carolyn Piper on August 20, 1996 what installations the Chairman was interested in, since he had told congressional leaders, "We have interests in Panama." Ms. Piper advised, "We can't discuss specific bases, as nothing has firmed up; only a U.S. presence after 1999 has been discussed." Just what is wrong with telling the American people what bases are needed is unclear.

U.S. Department of Defense representative Lt. Col. Arne Owens told me on August 21, 1996 that it may be "early" to plan post-1999 details for Panama. Nonetheless, some reports suggest that "time has virtually run out on the feasibility of getting the U.S. Congress to modify the Treaties ...the Pentagon having already 'zeroed out' funding for Panama after 1999" (The Washington Post, Douglas Farah, "Panama Makes Plans for U.S. Installations," July 28, 1996).

We should also note that Panamanian newspaper El Panama America reported on May 20, 1996, "For Pentagon officials, the talks should not be postponed beyond June, 1996 because the DOD is already preparing its budget estimates for the year 2000." Obviously, dawdling on both sides is going to cramp planning and negotiations for any U.S. bases in Panama.

CHAPTER 4

Panama Bases for Negotiation

The exploratory talks were scheduled for November 30, 1995, but were postponed at Panama's request, apparently so Panama could consolidate its position. Although public opinion polls definitely favor U.S. bases, some Panamanian leaders oppose the idea, namely: Catholic Bishop Jesus Ariz, former La Prensa publisher Roberto Eisenmann, National Assembly President Balbina Herrera and former Canal Administrator Fernando Manfredo, to name a few. The purpose of the exploratory talks is to find out if there is sufficient interest on the part of both nations to move on to formal negotiations.

The New York Times and The Washington Post have carried brief stories about these proposed talks, pointing out that as the time approaches for Canal transfer, the Panamanians seem to be getting nervous about the United States bases since they have incomplete plans for the use of all of them. The Times even hinted that the U.S. military is "watching them squirm."

Resolutions for continuing bases

Senator Helms and Congressmen Crane and Pickett introduced, and obtained many co-sponsors for resolutions demanding continuation of U.S. bases to defend the Panama Canal. Prior to 1994, these resolutions died in Democratic-controlled committees, but after Republicans took over the Congress in 1994, some progress was made.

The House Subcommittee on the Western Hemisphere under Chairman Dan Burton, R-Ind., held hearings on Congressman Crane's H. Con. Res. 4, a non-binding "sense of the Congress" measure. In his testimony, Crane recommended a landlord-tenant arrangement for the Canal and the bases.

Let us note also that General Barry McCaffrey, SOUTHCOM's Commander-in-Chief, changed his mind about the importance of the bases. His position in May 1995, according to high staff members, was that U.S. interest could be handled outside Panama. But on August 17, 1995, he said, "The United States should renegotiate the military bases..." The Clinton-Balladares agreement for exploratory talks followed.

Would bases violate Treaties?

Some opponents to continuing U.S. bases in Panama after 1999 charge that such action would violate the Panama Canal Treaties. This is untrue and needs to be cleared up. On the contrary, the Nunn Condition to the Treaties (Condition (2) U.S. Instrument—Neutrality Treaty) specifies that the two countries may negotiate for the "stationing of any United States military forces or the maintenance of defense sites," as both countries deem "necessary or appropriate."

Moreover, the U.S. implementing legislation, Section 1111 of the Panama Canal Act of 1979, specifies: "It is the sense of the Congress that the President enter into negotiations with the Republic of Panama for the purpose of arranging for the stationing of United States military forces, after the termination of the Panama Canal Treaty of 1977...and for the maintenance of installations and facilities, after the termination of such treaty, for the use of United States military forces stationed in such area."

Clearly, both the Neutrality Treaty and the U.S. implementing bill provide for negotiated arrangements between Panama and the United States for U. S. military installations after 1999.

Which military bases?

Some facts and justification on the specific U.S. military installations in Panama recommended for negotiation are in order:

1. **Howard Air Force Base,** on the Pacific side, is a 5,300 acre all-weather jet air base and home of the 24th Air Wing of the U.S. Air Force, operating fighters and interceptors, helicopters, transports, surveillance AWACs and cargo planes, with an 8,000 foot runway, strong enough to handle any plane that flies, including the C-5. It is probably the largest and most important U.S. base south of the Rio Grande. Its operators engage in drug interdiction in the war against illegal narcotics, air traffic operations, rescue missions and pilot training.

2. **Rodman Naval Station,** also on the Pacific side, is a deep-draft port facility, capable of handling any warship for logistic support in supplies, fueling and limited repairs. Its piers and other facilities are operating first class.

3. **Fort Sherman,** on the Atlantic side, is unique in that it is the only base in the world specializing in jungle warfare and survivor training. As with Howard AFB and

Rodman NS, Fort Sherman is another magnificent military installation, developed by dedicated professionals, loyal to their mission and proficient in its execution.

4. **Galeta Island,** also on the Atlantic side, is a very important intelligence-collecting and code- breaking facility for SOUTHCOM, indeed for the United States. Many details of its operations are classified, but it is known that the location is unique in its geological properties for underwater communication in both the Atlantic and Pacific Oceans and for collecting important intelligence.

5. **Quarry Heights Headquarters** for SOUTHCOM is a well-established and fully outfitted facility, sitting on Ancon Hill in Panama near the Gorgas Army Hospital and Ancon Hill Communications antenna array. This superb headquarters layout—now flying both the United States and Panamanian flags—is scheduled for surrender to Panama on October 1, 1998. New SOUTHCOM headquarters will be built at Miami according to current plans, far from the on-scene operations. This is alleged to be a "better location " by SOUTHCOM staff. Why? Well, some of Latin American countries do not feel comfortable in doing business with SOUTHCOM in Panama. Is this a real reason? Will all this be paid for by some newly discovered federal money tree that we've not heard about?

6. **Ancon Hill Communications** is SOUTHCOM's million-dollar antenna arrays on top of Ancon Hill, visible for miles around and capable of world-spanning communications. The plan is to transfer it to Panama and build another near the new headquarters in Miami.—all paid for, apparently, from the aforementioned federal money tree.

These then are the six U.S. military installations recommended for negotiations from the "informal talks" agreed to by Presidents Clinton and Balladares at their White House meeting of September 6, 1995.

Panama's business sector backs bases

Another interesting development, since the May, 1995 "Mission to Panama," was the report of strong backing of U.S. bases by Panamanian business interests, as publicized in the August 27, 1995 edition of Panamanian newspaper El Panama America.

This support by Panama's business sector was exactly in line with my proposal to officials of the Panama-area Chamber of Commerce on May 3, 1995 during our conference in Panama that the Chamber poll its 1,200 members to ask support of continuing some of the U.S. bases after 1999 and further, to poll members about whether President Balladares should suggest negotiations with the United States for future base rights.

Importance of the bases

A friend of mine, a World War II hero and winner of the Navy Cross for exceptional bravery, noted our campaign for saving some of the bases in Panama. He wrote me, "To Hell with Panama—all they want is money from bases—and further problems for us!" Well, I've been thinking about this criticism from this intelligent and proven patriot, and decided for myself:

The price of national security is not cheap and its problems are not small. Investment in sound security and American interests at the Isthmus of Panama must not be glossed over or dismissed out of hand. They remain important issues.

CHAPTER 5

Fact Finding in Panama

Our 1995 "Mission to Panama" was extensive—a follow-up to our 1994 Mission with conservative leader Howard Phillips, Representative Phil Crane, R-Ill., and other observers. We covered a lot of territory and obtained valuable information. Many people helped with arrangements. The following "Thank You" is from the President of the National Security Center, Richard A. Delgaudio:

> I would like to take the opportunity to thank those in Panama who contributed to the success of this "Mission" and to the continuation of friendship and shared interests between the peoples of Panama and our country. Vaya con Dios (go with God), to Panama City's Mayor Mayin Correa D., Dr. Jorge Eduardo Ritter, Ray Bishop, Jose Ramon Varela C., Victor A. Ortiz T., Captain Ralph Mendenhall, Dr. Ruben Carles, Juan Correa, Alonzo Fernandez, Maria Cristina Ozores T., Ricardo A. Morcillo C., Luis Rivera, Brig. Gen. Richard Brown III, Dr. Carlos Mendoza, Gabriel Lewis Galindo and especially, Ray Bishop. for making our emissary, Captain Evans, welcome in your country. I thank you all.

Surprise from General Colin Powell

One of the astonishing findings of my seven day fact finding mission to Panama, during the period May 1-7, 1995, was the comment by former President Guillermo Endara (1990-1994) that Chairman Colin Powell of the U.S. Joint Chiefs of Staff had told him that the United States was pulling out in 1999 and would not need bases, including Howard Air Force Base, for defense and drug interdiction.

This statement by General Powell apparently caused President Endara to switch his position because he told me, on April 6, 1994 (last year's "Mission to Panama") in the Presidential Palace, that his official position was "neutral," but that when he left office on August 31, 1994, he could go public in supporting U.S. bases after 1999, the Treaty surrender date.

Panamanians favor U.S. bases

Even with the disappointment of President Endara's apparent change of heart, a staggering 83 percent of the 31 political, military, business, media and labor leaders interviewed and expressing opinions during our 1995 trip favored continuing some of the U.S. bases after 1999—up from 79 percent in 1994. Moreover, a Dichter & Neira poll of 1214 Panamanians on May 6-7, 1995, had public opinion favoring U.S. bases 75.6 percent—up from 71 percent in a 1994 poll by La Prensa, Panama's leading newspaper.

In the United States, a 1994 poll by Marketing Research Institute had 65.5 percent of Americans polled in favor of bases.

Publicity for our Mission

All members of our group participated in the interviews. We traveled over 300 miles around Panama City. We were met by TV cameras for an interview about our mission. Later in the week, it was the popular "Breakfast in Panama" show with host Hugo Famania where we again explained our mission and identified the people we'd interviewed.

Fortunately, these two TV programs were beamed throughout Panama and thousands of Panamanians learned the views of NSC supporters on U.S. bases. It was a unique opportunity.

Interviews by Panamanian newspapers

At our interview on May 5, 1995 with La Estrella de Panama, one of the country's largest newspapers, we were welcomed by owner Maria Cristina Ozores T. and staff members, whom we briefed in detail about our mission to: (1) support Congressman Crane's Resolution, and (2) publicize Panamanian and American citizens' overwhelming 3-to-1 solidarity in support of mutual security via U.S. bases, according to polls in both countries.

Owner Ozores T. served refreshments and promised a front page story with photos for Sunday, May 7. Later, on May 24 in Norfolk, Va., I received copies of this excellent coverage, just as promised.

At our interview on May 3 with General Manager

Juan Correa of La Prensa, we learned that former publisher Roberto Eisenmann had written that no U.S. bases and "not a single U.S. soldier" are needed to defend the Canal after 1999. Is Mr. Eisenmann prophetic? It is still a dangerous world. Nonetheless, Mr. Correa was interested in preserving some bases, saying, "I don't doubt need for protection at the Isthmus."

The La Prensa poll on bases of May 6-7, 1995, by pollster Dichter & Neira was published in the May 16 issue of the paper and revealed some startling information that may have surprised Mr. Eisenmann: 75.6 percent favored bases; 71.1 percent thought the Panama economy could not absorb jobs lost by base closings and 68.5 percent thought the U.S. military improved Panama's stability. Of the 21 questions asked, nearly all answers, in varying degrees, favored the Americans.

Now for a few specifics about some of the interviews with the 31 Panamanians and Americans representing, I believe, the most important leaders in Panama:

Panamanian political leaders

Panamanian Foreign Minister Gabriel Lewis Galindo, on May 2 repeated several times, "Ask for bases if you want them." Dr. Jorge Ritter, legal adviser to President Ernesto Balladares, added, "We are waiting for a formal request from you." Neither Galindo nor Ritter indicated any objection to the Crane proposal for a landlord-tenant arrangement.

President Balladares told me in 1994, "I'll do what the people want; I'm willing to sit down and talk bases." Unfortunately, during my 1995 visit, I could not follow-up because our "cut and dried" agreed-to appointment for May 2 at 2:30 p.m. was canceled at the last moment—after clearing the guards and x-rays detectors—because of a "presidential emergency."

The Mayor of Panama City, Mayin Correa D., more than made up for the Endara disappointment. She received us in City Hall on May 4 and proved to be an enthusiastic supporter of the bases, "I'm all for it!" She emphatically pointed out the benefits in jobs, the economy and the defense of Panama. She was much concerned about the loss of jobs by citizens of Panama City.

Dr. Ruben Carles, a leading 1994 presidential candidate, was outspoken in advocating bases, but added that the United States should ask and commence negotiating.

Dr. Carlos Mendoza, President of the Interoceanic Region Authority (ARI) in charge of planning use of the "reverted" U.S. properties, explained the difficulties of handling so much so fast. Personally, he approved continuing some bases, but said ARI took no position.

Former President of the National Assembly, Alonzo Fernandez, is a strong supporter of U.S. bases and recommended Howard, Rodman, Fort Sherman and Galeta Island.

U.S. military leaders

Brig. General Richard E. Brown III, U.S. Air Force, Commander 24th Air Wing, likes the Crane-proposed landlord-tenant idea, saying, "It works in other places." Moreover, he noted, the drug interdiction program of Howard AFB is very important and "could not be done better anywhere else." The electronics network at Howard is the "central brain" of the U.S. Southern Command (SOUTHCOM). Is Howard important for SOUTHCOM's mission? "Absolutely!"

Captain Arthur N. Rowley III, U. S. Navy, Commanding Officer of Rodman Naval Station, says Rodman's functions could be "farmed out" to commercial interests at Balboa, but admits they can be done better at Rodman where piers and facilities are already operating shipshape. Rodman's importance to the Navy is indicated by its surrender date: December 31, 1999.

Lt. Colonel Richard Nazario, U.S. Army, Deputy Director of the Center for Treaty Implementation, and Major Joseph C. Myers, U.S. Army, Panama Canal Treaty officer, gave us an excellent briefing and interview on May 2 about Treaty implementation, as indicated in a schedule of U.S. installations, Appendix E.

The announced move of SOUTHCOM headquarters from Quarry Heights, Panama to Miami was discussed. Miami was called a "better location" because, allegedly, some of the Latin American Countries hesitate to do business with SOUTHCOM when located in Panama.

Questions: Are these legitimate reasons? How can a location remote from the scene of operations be an improvement? What's wrong with the excellent SOUTHCOM headquarters already operating on Quarry Heights? Why not try to negotiate under the Nunn Condition of the Panama Canal Treaty? How about the millions of dollars worth of antenna arrays being abandoned on Ancon Hill? Is there some new federal money tree that we've not heard about?

Panamanian business and labor leaders

Mr. Fernando Eleta, a former negotiator of the proposed 1967 Panama Canal Treaties, and former Foreign Minister, told us on May 3 that drug interdiction was no excuse for keeping Howard AFB open, the Canal could not be defended and the Communist threat was over. Our answer: It is still a dangerous world and defense against evil-doers is prudent.

Mr. Raymond B. Underwood of Levonel, Inc. shocked us on May 5 with his report of young men drilling in the early morning hours along the Flamenco Causeway chanting Noriega slogans. The rise of militarism? As for the U.S. bases, he urged, "Negotiate without delay!"

Chamber of Commerce officials Jose Ramon Varela C., Victor A. Ortiz, and Paola A. Valdez favored negotiating bases, as did the Chamber's Board of Directors, representing 1200 members. They agreed to poll their membership about bases and whether Panama's National Assembly should ask the U.S. to negotiate-and publicize results. Later, we found out the chamber did!

Mr. Ray Bishop, former secretary-general of local union 907 and 1994 candidate for the National Assembly, in our May 6 interview, cited potential job losses if all U.S. bases close, 12,000 total. He noted that 3,000 jobs would be saved if Howard, Rodman, Fort Sherman and Galeta Island remain open. Mr. Bishop stated that he always supported the U.S. military and its presence in Panama, for which he had been threatened. Nonetheless, he continues to do what he believes is right.

Panama Canal Commission

Mr. Raymond P. Laverty, Deputy Administrator, and Mr. James Ferrara, Director of the Canal Transition Commission, in our May 3 interview, saw no difficulty in future Canal operations by Panama since the Canal is the "heart" of the nation and will be carefully attended. Mr. Ferrara noted delays by Panama in accepting some of the "reverted" properties, but believes Panama "will inherit a well-run Canal."

U.S. Embassy

The following U.S. Embassy personnel were interviewed on May 3: Economic Counselor Elizabeth Bollman, Political Counselor Carol van Voorst and Labor Counselor John Mohanco.

Tape recorders and cameras were not allowed inside the Embassy and security was especially tight. The Counselors were committed to a rigid implementation of the Treaties and had no comment on any need to continue any of the U.S. bases. They did, however, admit to optimism that the Crane landlord-tenant deal for bases might work. Ms. Carol van Voorst commented that the Treaties were a fait accompli and that any difference in versions did not matter.

I pointed out, as I did last year when the same issue came up, that the non-acceptance by Panama of the DeConcini Reservation guaranteeing unilateral U.S. defense rights and U.S. non-acceptance of Panama's counter-reservation requiring "mutual cooperation" for any Canal defense, could be the source of some future acrimony and misunderstanding between our countries- and that these differences should be resolved now by renegotiating those portions of the Treaties.

Conclusions of the 1995 Mission

• Of the leaders who expressed opinions, 83 percent favored bases after 1999 and 17 percent opposed- all in line with polls.

• The Crane Resolution (H. Con. Res. 4) should be voted on by the House and Senate and attached to another bill and passed by the Congress.

• The Panamanian National Assembly probably will not pass a resolution for a plebiscite for U.S. bases. It is up to the United States to initiate discussion to save the U.S. bases.

• The Panamanians are facing a crisis in the dumping of U.S. bases before Panama has adequately planned for their use. Retention of several bases by the U.S. would help resolve this crisis.

• Nearly all leaders interviewed favored Howard Air Force Base, Rodman Naval Station, Fort Sherman and Galeta Island as the proper bases for the United States to retain.

Panama's leaders in 1995 were clearly ready to negotiate in friendship and in good faith for mutual self-interest, to retain some of the U.S. bases after 1999, preferably Howard Air Force Base, Rodman Naval Station, Fort Sherman and Galeta Island.

Time is running out to preserve the national security interests of the United States at Panama, and the security interests of Panama and the entire hemisphere for a secure Panama Canal, judged by Admiral Thomas Moorer to be the "most vital strategic waterway in the entire world."

CHAPTER 6

Finally: Hearing on Crane Resolution

With the surrender date for the Panama Canal fast approaching, December 31, 1999, interest in preserving several U.S. military installations in Panama after 1999 has increased. On January 4, 1995, Congressman Philip M. Crane, R.-Ill., introduced his House Concurrent Resolution 4 (H. Con. Res. 4) for the purpose of negotiating a new base rights agreement with the Republic of Panama and for permitting the United States to "act independently to continue to protect the Canal."

In years past, the Crane Resolution grew steadily in popularity, gaining 85 co-sponsors in 1994, with 17 Democrats joining 68 Republicans. The number was expected to grow and the chances good that hearings would be held before the House Subcommittee on Western Hemisphere Affairs, chaired by Representative Dan Burton, R-Ind., a stalwart Republican and long-time critic of the 1977 Panama Canal Treaties. Western Hemisphere Affairs is a subcommittee of the House Committee on International Relations, chaired by Representative Benjamin A. Gilman, R-NY.

Value of Canal on the rise

The economic value of the Canal is going to increase because of the new NAFTA and GATT international trade agreements which have reduced tariffs and increased trade in the region. The strategic value of the

Canal is increasing because of the downsizing of the U.S. Navy to almost 50 percent. Without a two-ocean Navy, the Canal is vital for rapid transfer of warships ocean to ocean.

With its strategic and economic value increasing, the Canal is also becoming more and more a tempting target for the terrorists of the world. Critics have long claimed that the Canal is indefensible. This is ludicrous. Would the Canal be more, or less, defensible with no U.S. bases nearby? Did the United States abandon the "indefensible" canal to Adolph Hitler and to Japan during World War II? Today, the defense and security of this vital chokepoint is more vital than at any time in the Canal's history.

Can the unstable and weak government of Panama handle this situation alone, with only a police force since its armed forces have been abolished? Even a strong and prosperous Panama could use the help of the United States in some kind of partnership—the world still has big bullies as well as sneaky terrorists, and who better to help contain such problems than Uncle Sam?

A permanent U.S. military presence would best serve Panamanian and U.S. interests. Otherwise, the vacuum created by a U.S. withdrawal would quickly be filled-possibly by China, Japan or a United Nations force. What irony!

Is there anyone in America who thinks that vital U.S. strategic interests will be protected and defended by Chinese, Japanese or United Nations troops? Remember, in the case of the latter, we are talking about the troops which have so far failed to stabilize small European and African war-torn nations. What would happen at the Panama Canal if vital U.S. strategic and even economic interest (i.e., the crippling of the U.S. economy) were at stake as terrorists or even an armed revolutionary brigade attempted to close the Canal by violent means?

Some say U.S. interests are protected by the U.S. DeConcini Reservation to the Panama Canal Treaties which would authorize unilateral U.S. defense of the Canal after 1999. Not quite. Senator Dennis DeConcini's Reservation, as amended (or canceled to put it more bluntly) by Panama's counter-reservation, requires "cooperation," and "cooperation" was the stipulation secretly inserted into the Treaties and never agreed to by the U.S. Senate. Future discord is almost guaranteed by this major discrepancy in the Treaties.

The point is: What if Panama, for any reason, decides it does not choose to "cooperate"? If U.S. critical national interests are involved, an invasion could be the result. What then would those who claim, "We have defense rights," have to say about such a situation? "Oh," they'd say, "we thought we had that. Sorry." Sorry is right, but it's too little, too late and too bad.

Polls favor U.S. bases

Public opinion polls taken in 1994 both in Panama and in the United States favor 3 to 1 continuing some U.S. military installations in Panama after 1999. One would expect, therefore, that the governments of both nations would quickly negotiate. Not so, even though modern leaders always say they do what the people want. Panamanian leaders, including President Balladares, say, in effect, "It's up to you (the U.S.)," preferring not to be perceived as asking any favors of the giant to the north.

This view of the Panamanians, was clearly evident during my April, 1994 interviews in Panama with 27 political, labor and business leaders when 79 percent of those questioned wanted the United States to retain some of its military installations after 1999. One of the main reasons the Panamanians want "Yanqui, stay here," replacing the old slogan of "Yanqui, go home" is clearly economic. According to one report, the "Yanquis" had been pouring some $206 million per year into Panama's economy, almost six percent of its $3.9 billion economy. Another reason is security of the Canal and of the government of Panama itself.

For example, former President Guillermo Endara called on the U.S. military early in his administration(1990-1994) to put down a coup attempt by Colonel Ernesto Herrera of the Panamanian Police Force. In late 1994, during the Balladares administration, the U.S. military had to quell riots by Cuban refugees being detained in Panama. Who will do these jobs if U.S. troops leave? Perhaps Red Chinese troops will be invited into Panama to "help out" in the future. Perhaps "combat" veterans of the Tienneman Square massacre will be brought in—so much better when the professionals with experience at maintaining order do their work.

Burton Subcommittee hears Crane

At long last we learn the Clinton position on future U.S. bases in Panama. It all happened on March 9, 1995, at the hearing on Congressman Philip M. Crane's, R-Ill. H. Con. Res. 4 before the House Subcommittee on the Western Hemisphere.

At best the position was lukewarm, despite public opinion polls in both countries favoring bases almost 3 to 1. Witness Anne Patterson, Deputy Assistant Secretary for InterAmerican Affairs, U.S. State Department, after a long harangue about the "structures and policies...necessary to continue viability of the Canal" and "optimum use of reverted properties," concluded, apparently with some reluctance, "that a limited U.S. troop presence in Panama would instill confidence in Canal users."

Hooray! Why not a kind word that U.S. troops might bolster and protect U.S. interests in the secure operation of the Canal and other concerns in the Southern Hemisphere—such as drug interdiction, promotion of democracy and jungle and survivor training of troops?

Defense Department lukewarm at hearing

The Department of Defense witness before this subcommittee was Frederick C. Smith, Principal Deputy Assistant Secretary for International Security Affairs. He was assisted by U.S. Army Brig. Gen. John R. Walsh, Assistant Deputy Director for Politico-Military Affairs JCS.

After a detailed run-down of regional interests, Southern Command missions and the Treaty Implementation Plan, Mr. Smith recognized that U.S. interests might be served after 1999 around Panama by holding onto a few bases.

He even quoted Section 1111 of the Panama Canal Act of 1979, the Treaties implementing legislation, that included a sense of Congress resolution declaring that "the best interests of the United States require that the President enter into negotiations with the Republic of Panama for the purpose of arranging for the stationing of United States military forces after the termination of the Panama Canal Treaty of 1977..." This was a follow-up to the Nunn Condition of the Treaty which said almost the same thing.

Nonetheless, before Mr. Smith signed off, he got in his little dig against "post-1999 basing" by saying he personally was comforted by the words of the Commander-in-Chief of the U.S. Southern Command who had said, "...we have no vital military or economic interests directly at stake in Panama which we cannot support through some other strategy."

Just what "strategy" was not disclosed. And just how the Canal could be defended and drugs interdicted from afar was not explained either. Wouldn't common sense tell us that nothing beats being on-scene to handle problems and missions? This wild claim might be popular in the corridors of the White House but is hardly responsive to concerns expressed by this author, by the watchdog National Security Center and by vigilant U.S. Senators and Congressman such as Senator Jesse Helms and Congressman Philip Crane.

Crane proposes owner-client deal

The strongest testimony at this hearing came from Congressman Crane who was there to defend his concurrent resolution (H. Con. Res. 4) calling for a base-rights and Canal-rights agreement to be negotiated.

This Crane proposal would be a business-like arrangement between the United States and Panama wherein the host country, Panama, would be owner and landlord of the Canal and bases—and the client state would be the United States which would be the tenant and operator of the facilities under the terms of the lease agreement. Moreover, the United States could maintain the facilities and provide security, depending on the terms of the agreement. Sovereignty would, of course, remain with Panama, as established by the Panama Canal Treaty.

Representative Crane went further, saying, "Also, since Panama does not have an army, the deal could include other things such as a U.S. commitment to defend all of Panama from attack, not just the Canal."

Other benefits of the Crane proposition are self-evident, for example: Panama would be collecting rent money for the facilities, would be saving thousands of jobs that Panamanians now hold on the U.S. bases and would be preserving millions of dollars of its economy annually—the amount now spent by U.S. forces in Panama.

Advantages to United States

The advantages to the United States are also substantial, despite the qualms expressed above by the State and Defense Departments, as follows: (1) Use of the military installations would allow us to carry out Southern Command's missions, drug interdiction and Canal defense more efficiently, and (2) the benefits of increased commerce generated by the GATT and NAFTA trade agreements would be considerable both for the United States and for the countries in the region.

Apparently for the above economic and security reasons, both Panamanians and Americans strongly favored U.S. bases in Panama after 1999. Public opinion polls have proved this point. Congressman Crane asks, "What are we waiting for?" Then, he offers a sensible solution to resolve the matter.

Impasse of who asks first

Panamanian leaders did not want to ask first. Several of them told me as much when I talked with them on my last National Security Center funded Mission to Panama, saying, in effect, "It's up to you (the U.S.) to ask." President Guillermo Endara told me that, as did President-elect Ernesto "Toro" Balladares. Congressman Crane said, "I think we should take the first step and call for the negotiation of a base and Canal-rights agreement."

This "first step" could be to vote congressional approval of legislation or a resolution such as Crane's H. Con. Res. 4, calling on President Clinton to negotiate. Then, the pressure would be on President Clinton to act, perhaps even overcoming his reluctance to move against a major campaign contributor (Red China's government) which has interest in moving into the vacuum left by the United States' inaction. Unfortunately, the House Subcommittee on Western Hemisphere did not vote. I asked Chairman Dan Burton, R-Ind., to call for a vote, but received no answer.

Perhaps Congressman Burton, a stalwart conservative on so many other important issues, feels this matter is not a priority. So much rides on whether interested and informed Americans, such as the readers of this book, take the time to write letters and circulate information about this issue to friends and neighbors, write letters to the editor, speak out on radio talk shows and donate to organizations such as the National Security Center.

Other witnesses before the Subcommittee that day included Congressman Gene Taylor, D-Miss.; Colonel John A. Cope, a Senior Fellow with the Institute for National Strategic Studies at the National Defense University; and Dr. Richard Millet, Director for National Programs with the North-South Center—all of whom were apparently in general agreement with the advantage of some kind of U.S. presence in Panama after the Canal is surrendered in 1999.

Stand-down of U.S. forces

The "stand down" of forces in Panama was proceeding quite rapidly with some 50 percent scheduled by the end of 1995. Time is of the essence for negotiating an agreement with Panama. Now that the Panamanians have their long-cherished Panama Canal Treaty, they are not ready for the consequences involved in the turnover of huge bases and facilities. Indeed, many of those already turned over are in a state of disrepair—deteriorated, rusted out and generally neglected. The turnover is nearing "the point of no return," say Representative Crane, meaning that rejuvenation and repair of neglected facilities will soon not be practicable. I photographed some of the deteriorating U.S. property turned over to the Panamanians on an earlier National Security Center funded "Mission to Panama"—namely the Panama Railroad which runs roughly parallel to the Canal. The railroad was rendered completely inoperable once it was turned over to the Panamanians by the United States. Is Panama better off having 100% control of the Canal?

Questions about SOUTHCOM's move to Miami

The move of our Southern Military Command (SOUTHCOM in military parlance) from Panama to Miami was actively downplayed by the Clinton Administration and hardly even noted by the news media. But questions abound—questions which should be asked by concerned citizens—especially in writing to their U.S. Senators, their Congressmen, in letters to the editor, in radio talk shows. Those questions include:

• Is this a practicable location for controlling and directing operations in the Southern Hemisphere, despite the tremendous capabilities of modern technology?

• Would Panama be a good "on-scene" location for SOUTHCOM's headquarters, i.e., closer to the action involved in defending the Canal and interdicting drugs, for example?

• Is the proposed move to Miami designed to forestall critics who want the headquarters to remain in Panama, i.e., make the move a fait accompli, thereby making it much harder or impossible to hold onto the Quarry Heights headquarters?

Besides, millions of U.S. taxpayers dollars have already been invested in the Quarry Heights headquarters and in the Ancon Hill antenna array. Why scrap all this and spend another fortune building another SOUTHCOM headquarters and communications facility in Miami? The Miami taxpayers will love it. But how about the other taxpayers in the U.S.A.?

The State and Defense witnesses before Chairman Burton's subcommittee were saying in the best governmentese that consideration for future U.S. base rights in Panama was "under study." These Departments have had 16 years to study this issue—since 1979! Give us a break.

This striking aerial photo shows the 3-step Gatun Locks on the Atlantic side of the Canal, looking South into Gatun Lake, the largest man-made lake in the world at the time of its creation 1908-1914. Gatun Locks, double-chambered, lifts South-bound ships 85 feet into Gatun Lake and lowers North-bound ships 85 feet into the Caribbean Sea. These Locks are flanked by earthen dams, largest in the world when constructed in 1910-1912. (Photo/Panama Canal Commission)

In the center is the famous landmark, the Panama Canal administration building, housing the officials who operate the Canal and generations of momentous historical events. In the background is Panama City with its dozens of shining white-faced high-rise buildings—constructed, many say, with "drug money," an impressive sight. (Photo/Panama Canal Commission)

This aerial view of Pedro Miguel Locks looks North towards Gaillard Cut in the Continental Divide. Pedro Miguel is a 1-step lock that lifts ships 34 feet North-bound and lowers them 34 feet South-bound. Pedro Miguel would be removed in a "Terminal Lake-Third Locks Plan" proposed by the late Captain Miles P. DuVal, U.S. Navy, to expand the capacity of the Canal and improve safety and navigation. (Photo/Panama Canal Commission)

Miraflores Locks on the Pacific side is in 2-steps and has a 51-foot lifting/lowering capacity. Under the DuVal-proposed plan, these locks would be converted to 3-steps, just as Gatun locks are. (Photo/Panama Canal Commission)

A Maersk Lines container ship makes its way through the Canal. South-bound from Gatun Locks, one of many Maersk ships that save some 8,000 miles and 18 days steaming time with each transit, as compared to the Cape Horn route—savings of millions of dollars annually for steamship companies such as Maersk. (Photo/Panama Canal Commission)

This ship in entering Gaillard Cut from Gatun Lake, South-bound. This Cut, formerly Culebra Cut, was named for Lt. Colonel David D. Gaillard, U.S. Army, in charge of the excavation through the Continental Divide, the toughest job in digging the Canal. The Cut is 8 miles long, originally 312 feet above sea-level, and had 168 million cubic yards of dirt and rocks excavated—enough to circle the Earth four times, yard-to-yard. (Photo/Panama Canal Commission)

The Colombia M/V CURACAO REEFER, approaching Miraflores Locks North-bound in this May 1996 photo, is somewhat typical of the South American water-borne commerce that depends on the Canal. Article VI of the Neutrality Treaty authorizes toll-free transits for the "troops, vessels and materials of war" of Colombia and Costa Rica. Both nations border Panama; and Panama was once a province of Colombia. (Photo/Panama Canal Commission)

CHAPTER 7

Integrity: a Key Ingredient

Integrity is the key ingredient not much seen in the manipulations and maneuvers that produced the Treaties for surrender of the Canal and U.S. bases to the Republic of Panama. For example, if integrity had mattered, the Democratic Treaties manager in the U.S. Senate, Senator Paul Sarbanes, D—Md., would never have allowed a major change to the Treaties, Panama's counter-reservation, to by-pass without a vote. If integrity had mattered to Dictator Omar Torrijos of Panama, he would have held a plebiscite for approval of the six major changes added by the United States as required by Article 274 of his Constitution. So much for integrity in the Panama Treaties.

Integrity must certainly be an ingredient in the operation, condition and reliability of the Canal itself. A partnership, similar to the Panama Canal Commission, would seem to assure world commerce of continuing a smoothly operating and well-maintained Panama Canal.

The condition of this 83-year old Canal is a prime consideration and again, integrity is a factor—honesty with customers and absolute reliability of service. Honesty with the public about the condition of the Canal calls for integrity, rather then shielding reports that may be "political and sensitive," as was done by the Panama Canal Commission with the April 1996 U.S. Army Corps of Engineers "Operations and Maintenance Study." This study, reprinted by National Security Center, found the Canal "wearing out...due to lack of main-tenance caused by the need to lock ships."

The media have a very important role in integrity to inform the public about developments concerning the Canal and its infrastructure. One-sided press articles and television programs are unfair, particularly with "stars" who do not know the subject and , who, in many cases, are being "politically correct" at the expense of the truth in protecting the champions of these unconstitutional Treaties.

Integrity of the Constitution

One of the four major goals of the U.S. action in 1989 against Manuel Antonio Noriega was "to preserve the integrity of the Panama Treaties"—and to continue "as long as it takes." May we include the integrity of the Constitution of the United States? As a priority?

President Bush knew of the increasing allegations concerning the 1977 Treaties. He and key members of his staff, as well as all 100 senators, 232 U.S. representatives and members of the major media all have received documented proof of the unconstitutional procedures used by the Carter Administration in "ratifying" these Treaties. The Military Order of the World Wars (DC Chapter) sponsored delivery to these people of the book, The Panama Canal Treaties Swindle: Consent to Disaster (Signal Books), containing the shocking story, with a cover letter from four top military strategists, including former chairman of the Joint Chiefs of Staff Admiral Tom Moorer, and the late General Albert C. Wedemeyer.

So why is corrective action not taken? It's a deep secret major media are happy to keep. The Washington

Administration, the media and other sympathizers obviously prefer the status quo, i.e., don't bother us with legitimate United States rights in Panama.

Panama's secret counter-reservation

The swindle of the Canal, if it is consummated, has a dozen separate parts, chief of which is the Carter Administration's failure to submit Panama's secret three-paragraph counter-reservation to the Senate for a vote, as specified by Article II of our Constitution. Appendix A contains these three paragraphs, as copied from Panama's Instruments of Ratification of the Panama Canal Treaty. They were called "the most substantive change imaginable" by the late Charles H. Breecher, one of the State Departments most knowledgeable treaty experts.

In the second paragraph of this counter-reservation is the phrase, "mutual respect and cooperation," meaning that Panama's "cooperation" is required before the United States can act the defend or open the Canal, thereby killing the U.S. DeConcini Reservation that had guaranteed unilateral U.S. defense rights.

A solution has been suggested by the veteran strategist Dr. Robert Morris, Chairman of the America's Future organization. U.S. senators owe taxpayers one: let them vote on the counter-reservation now.

If approved by a two-thirds vote, both sets of Treaties would be identical and Article II of the Constitution complied with. But, the DeConcini Reservation would be dead and consequently, U.S. unilateral defense rights non-existent. But if the Senate disapproved Panama's counter-reservation, the DeConcini Reservation would remain in full force and U.S. defense rights assured constitutionally.

The integrity of the U.S. Constitution, therefore, is far more important that the "integrity of the Panama Treaties"—and a proper vote on Panama's counter-reservation is a first step towards constitutional Panama Canal Treaties. For the record, let us note that other parts of the U.S. Constitution, Panama's Constitution, and the Vienna Convention of the Law of Treaties 1969 were also violated.

Why not a partnership to run the Canal?

One solution to the illegal 1977 Panama Treaties and the unsettling prospect of turning over this great strategic waterway to the unstable government of Panama in 1999 may be a very simple agreement to continue the present arrangement: a permanent Panama Canal Commission of United States and Panamanian directors to operate the Canal as partners.

Negotiating treaties outlining a permanent partnership between the two countries with provisions for U.S. base rights and Panamanian sovereignty could be best for all concerned.

There are a number of compelling reasons for developing a permanent partnership: Panama has no defense force as such, and no immediate plans and prospects for one, for the future defense of the Canal, while the United States, of course, is in place with adequate defense for the Canal and for Panama itself.

The 1977 Panama Treaties, according to many constitutional scholars of both countries, were "ratified" outside the U.S. Constitution and Panama's Constitution in several substantive instances.

The continuing argument about unconstitutional

Treaties could be solved and placed in the background, and emphasis placed on an operating partnership.

With the United States as a permanent partner, modernization of the Canal could be facilitated.

The United States, as an operating partner, could guarantee security of the Canal for U.S. interests, and protect Panama's interests and world commerce.

The threat of a future military dictatorship would be abolished by Panama's abolition of its army and by dependence on the United States for defense of the Canal and Panama itself.

In the interests of continuing the smooth operation of the complex Panama Canal system and assuring its continuing maintenance and operation, the formation of a continuing partnership is the practical solution.

'State-of-the-Canal'

The U.S. Army Corps of Engineers with a team of eleven experienced engineers, headed by Structural Engineer John C. Griber, spent several months in 1995 and 1996 studying the Canal infrastructure: "an operations and maintenance study...related to the transit operations and procedures."

This project, agreed to by both nations and instigated by the Board of Directors of the Panama Canal Commission, was to determine the "State-of-the-Canal," preparatory to surrender to Panama in 1999. After reviewing the Army's report, "Operations and Maintenance Study," the Board decided to call it "politically sensitive" and prohibited distribution to the media and other outsiders.

Mr. Griber briefed the Board and selected Panamanian government and business leaders on August 19,

1996 in Panama, saying, among other things, "[T]he Canal is operating efficiently" but "maintenance needs to be increased." Details of deteriorated concrete in the tunnels and lock chambers were apparently not discussed at that time.

The study itself reports: general condition of infrastructure "good," but replacement concrete needed in machinery tunnels at Gatun and Miraflores Locks, for example. Crumbling and cracked concrete was noted in other areas—replacement recommended.

Recommendations were also made for improving maintenance on miter gates, operating machinery, rising stem valves, the control system and power distribution—also for "making the SIP-7 Systems operable." These are the hydraulic systems designed to "guard against loss of pool," i.e., to prevent draining the Canal from bombs or terrorist attacks.

"Corrosion" and "deterioration" were the words used to describe most of the 83-year old Canal and infrastructure, and "good" and "very good" for over-all conditions of such items as the three locks, Miraflores Spillway, Madden Dam, Gatun Dam and the 25 saddle dams. Improvements costing approximately two billion dollars have been made since 1979, apparently as the PCC "deems appropriate" under the authority of Article III of the Panama Canal Treaty.

Another evaluation of the "State-of-the-Canal" was made by Bill Bright Marine, a dual citizen of Panama and the United States and an announced candidate for President of Panama in the 1999 elections. During his visit to Panama during the period July 7-14, 1996, he spent time at the Canal site, observing and talking with workers. He announced his candidacy for president, held news conferences and appeared on television and radio talk shows. He has "contacts." National Security

Center President Richard Delgaudio met with Mr. Marine in Florida twice to review his findings before sponsoring him for a briefing in Washington in 1997.

Mr. Marine's impression was that Canal maintenance was "not good," alleging that no Canal "major overhaul had been done in 17 years" and that the "SIP-7 Systems were not operating" because the "hydraulic fluid had been stolen and sold downtown." As for his sources, Mr. Marine said, "I have spent time talking to the workers who actually do the job in the locks and surrounding areas. They have told me horror stories. They also told me about the Corps of Engineers report. The problem is this modernization nonsense. The locks are in bad shape..." He calls for "major overhauls immediately."

In his discussions with me, Mr. Marine revealed that he favors a new Panama Canal Treaty that would provide for a U.S.—Panama partnership to operate the Canal plus preserving many U.S. bases.

In a letter to Hutchison Whampoa Ltd., the Chinese company operating the ports at each end of the Canal, Mr. Marine stated that , when he becomes president of Panama, he (Bill Bright Marine) would "cancel the contract (and) not refund your investment, nor any fees paid..."

Mr. Marine added, "Control of ports by a company that will soon be under the control of the Communist Chinese is unacceptable to the national security interest of Panama and the United States. It is no accident that as the U.S. leaves strategic areas, Hutchison is there to fill the void."

As for Marine's allegation about "no major overhaul," Senior Panama Canal Pilot Ralph Mendenhall, a veteran of over 3,000 accident-free transits of the Canal as pilot, says that the PCC does not do "major overhauls" because they would close-down locks chambers for several months, causing unacceptable back-ups in Canal traffic, whereas, the mini-overhauls are faster and eventually cover all necessary aspects of a "major overhaul." Yet in the past under U.S. control, major overhauls were done. One wonders.

Media integrity is questioned

The author has participated, as guest, on perhaps, a hundred radio talk shows and on several television shows, but nothing "big time." C-SPAN's Greg Barker said he wanted someone better known, such as, he said, "journalists and senators." Even though I explained that these are the very people who gave us the Panama swindle, Mr. Barker still wanted a star—never mind some upstart. Nonetheless, afterwards, in hearing journalists David Hess, Andrew Alexander and Tom Diemer on C-SPAN relegate the Monroe Doctrine as a relic of a "bygone era" and now dead, it appears that even C-SPAN is no longer after the truth, as moderator Brian Lamb quickly moved on to the next caller without questioning this presumptuous allegation by these media "stars."

The chill continued with my attempts to breach the walls into Good Morning America, Larry King Live and the Phil Donahue Show—and even onto my friend Pat Buchanan's Crossfire. But none of this will ever change the absolute fundamental that these Treaties are unconstitutional and must never be allowed to control the destiny of the Panama Canal.

CHAPTER 8

The Swindle in Plain Words—
Who Can Disprove It?

Much has been written and argued about the "Give-away Panama Treaties" and "justice for Panama"—but the fact is: the Treaties are not a "giveaway" or a "steal," they are a swindle—the deprivation of property and rights under false pretenses. And as for "justice," how about justice for the Americans?

The purpose of this chapter is to address the swindle head-on in plain words and to prove every point of the swindle beyond any doubt. We call it the swindle of the century. Who can name a greater fraud?

We note that no other author, to our knowledge, calls the Treaties a swindle. No other term fits! Swindle is the perfect assessment. Even State Department treaty specialist, the late Dr. Charles H. Breecher, called the Treaties, "the greatest fraud ever perpetrated against the United States Senate and against the American people."

As for the future fate of the Canal and U.S. bases, insufficient consideration has been given to establishing a partnership, similar to the Panama Canal Commission, with both countries respected partners on Panamanian sovereign territory. Even so, the American president should not hesitate to tell the world that the United States has a strong determination to respect the independence of all nations, but an equally strong determination that the legitimate interests of America shall not be set aside.

President Carter sets the tone

Candidate-for-president Jimmy Carter promised voters in 1976, "I'll never give up control of the Panama Canal"—saying this the last time on October 17, 1976 in the Waldorf-Astoria ballroom. He also promised many times, "I'll never lie to you." But when he got the votes, he did the exact opposite. His very first official act after inauguration on January 20, 1977 was to sign National Security Defense Memorandum #1 (NSDM #1) to commence negotiating away the Panama Canal.

NSDM #1 had been drawn up by Robert Pastor, then aide to Zbigniew Brzezinski, Carter's National Security Adviser. Let us note again that in 1994 Pastor became President Clinton's nominee for U.S. ambassador to Panama. But his name was withdrawn after scandalous information was provided to the Senate Foreign Relations Committee by the National Security Center, Washington-based civilian organization.

Now, to the Treaties and the swindle. There are two Panama Canal Treaties: (1) the Panama Canal Treaty that provides for the gradual surrender of the Canal and all U.S. installations in good working order by December 31, 1999; and, (2) the Neutrality Treaty that guarantees permanent neutrality and an open Canal for all nations.

Why the Treaties are a swindle

The Treaties are a swindle because they would deprive American taxpayers of their property, territory and rights under false pretenses—the dictionary definition of swindle—not a giveaway, not a steal, but a swindle—the worst possible way to lose something precious!

The Canal Zone and the Canal are U.S. property, bought and paid for four times: (1) $40 million to the French Canal Company (Compagnie Universelle Du Canal Interoceanique) for its assets; (2) $25 million to Colombia from which Panama gained independence in 1903; (3) $10 million in gold to the new Republic of Panama for the purchase of the 10 mile wide 50 mile long Panama Canal Zone—not to rent or to lease but to purchase—in order to build that Wonder of the World, the Panama Canal; and, (4) $4.7 million total to the 3,598 individual land owners and squatters in the Canal Zone in title fee simple with deeds. This was a total of $79.7 million of U.S. taxpayers' money—probably the most bought and paid for piece of real estate in history, and the Americans did it!

The Canal Zone is also U.S. territory—so ruled by the U.S. Supreme Court in the Wilson v. Shaw case in 1907, and again by the Fifth Circuit Court of Appeals in the United States v. Husband R. (Roach) case in 1971.

The U.S. taxpayers would also be deprived of their rights by the Panama Treaties—sovereign rights "to the entire exclusion of the exercise by the Republic of Panama of any such sovereign rights…"—quoting Article III of the original Hay-Buanau-Varilla Treaty.

So much for those who, like Jimmy Carter, claim, "We only rented the Canal Zone." The facts are: The 1903 Treaty uses the word "grant" 19 times, the word "sovereignty" 6 times, and the words "rent" or "lease" no times. We owned the Canal Zone; it was never rented!

The swindle includes false pretenses

Continuing our explanations of swindle: The Panama Treaties were "ratified" under three false pretenses:

1. Both nations made believe they had "ratified" the same Treaties. They had not. There were two versions: Panama's version contains a 3-paragraph counter-reservation, not in the U.S. version, that requires Panama's "cooperation" before any U.S. defense of the Canal that, the U.S. Senate believed, had been guaranteed by the U.S. DeConcini Reservation. Panama's counter-reservation, called the "most substantive change imaginable" by State Department treaty expert Dr. Charles H. Breecher, was not submitted to the Senate for a two-thirds vote of approval, a direct violation of Article II of the Constitution which requires such a vote for all treaties and, of course, changes to treaties. Incidentally, Senator Paul Sarbanes, D—Md., who at this writing is obstructing the Senate investigation of the Clinton Whitewater and Travelgate scandals, was in 1977-78 the Democratic Senate floor manager for the Panama Treaties. It was his duty to direct Senate attention to Panama's counter-reservation. He failed to do so. A later survey of senators by Phillip Harman, Chairman of the Committee for Better Panama and United States Relations, disclosed that eight senators who voted for the Treaties would not have approved the Treaties had they seen Panama's counter-reservation beforehand. So much for integrity.

2. Both nations had to violate their own constitution in order to get Treaties they could get in no other way: President Carter allowed violation of Article II, as explained above. He also allowed violations of Articles IV and VI. Article IV contains the "property clause," requiring the Congress (both House and Senate) to dispose of U.S. territory and property. Only the Senate and the President acted to dispose of the Canal Zone, a violation of Article IV, since the House of Representatives was deprived of its constitutional duty in disposing of

property. Article VI contains the "supremacy clause" which makes treaties equal to laws as the "supreme law of the land." Therefore, if treaties are equal to laws, they must be terminated in the same manner that laws are terminated—by a vote of both houses of Congress. The House of Representatives never voted to terminate the original 1903 Treaty with Panama, which, therefore, constitutionally remains in force. Thus, President Carter allowed Articles II, IV and VI to be violated.

Torrijos violated Panama's Constitution

Continuing with the second false pretense: Panamanian Dictator Omar Torrijos violated his 1972 Constitution in two instances: Article 163 requires the President to sign treaties, but Dictator Torrijos signed—not President Demetrio B. Lakas, who told me on February 7, 1990 in Panama when I asked him why he didn't sign the Treaties as required by his Constitution, "Oh, I told Omar to just go ahead and sign." So much for constitutional procedures in Panama!

Torrijos also violated Article 274 of Panama's Constitution by not submitting the six major changes added to the Treaties by the United States to a Panamanian plebiscite, as required of these major changes. He and President Carter wanted their Treaties, and a little inconvenience like constitutional procedures must not stand in the way of the handiwork of U.S. negotiators Ellsworth Bunker and Sol Linowitz, and Panamanian negotiators Romulo Escobar Bethancourt and Fernando Manfredo—all assisted in varying degrees by Mike Kozak and Cyrus Vance of the State Department, and Henry Kissinger, Zbigniew Brzezinski and Robert Pastor of the Carter Team.

The third false pretense

3. Both nations kept hidden Panama's counter-reservation until the last moment, June 16, 1978 in Panama City, Panama where Dictator Torrijos "ratified" unconstitutionally the Treaties with great fanfare. Only at that time did the U.S. State Department hand out press releases disclosing Panama's illegal counter-reservation, "the most substantive change imaginable," that had never been seen by the Senate. This was just one more instance of dishonesty. Then, of course, it was too late for the Senate to object. The senators had been mouse-trapped, and Senators Sarbanes and Robert C. Byrd, D-WV, Majority Leader, could revel in their clever victory. These, then, are the three false pretenses of the Canal swindle: two versions of the Treaties; extensive violations of both nations' constitutions; and, hiding Panama's counter-reservation until the last moment.

How about a lawsuit?

Another fundamental ethic was grossly violated: the arrogant disposal of the owners-taxpayers property by the trustees who haughtily, and with malicious afore-thought, ignored the wishes of 79 percent of the owners who opposed surrender of the Canal and Canal Zone, according to public opinion polls at the time. Clearly, the U.S. taxpayers are the owners; it was their money that had bought the Canal Zone and paid for construction of the Canal. Just as clearly, the trustees are Carter, Kissinger, Vance, Brzezinski, Pastor, Bunker, Linowitz, Sarbanes, Byrd and all the 68 senators who voted for the

Treaties. It can be argued that they violated their trust and committed malfeasance of office.

It can also be argued that a federal lawsuit can be instigated against these trustees for malfeasance in unlawfully and unconstitutionally depriving owners of their properties and rights. Some lawyers, of course, will argue: You have to have standing in court. What greater standing is needed than that millions of law-abiding, tax-paying citizens are being deprived of their property and rights under false pretenses by incompetent and uncaring trustees?

I asked Judge Robert H. Bork, former Supreme Court nominee, about this and he said, "You would not have standing." Other lawyers have told me that Judge Bork has a tendency toward a finding of "no standing," adding, "why not try it?" Why not? If the lawsuit loses, then the judges will have on their hands the loss of the Canal, not the citizens who tried. National Security Center President Richard Delgaudio agreed that, with the right attorney stepping forward, his organization would be delighted to test this idea in court.

Many accept Treaties and surrender

As previously noted, these facts and many other documented details are recorded in the pages of The Panama Canal Treaties Swindle: Consent to Disaster (Signal Books). No major facts have ever been disproved.

The advocates of the Treaties and surrender of the Canal, probably America's most proud possession, have not challenged the documented facts, perhaps for two reasons: (1) They can't, because the facts are solid; or, (2) They don't have to—because they have already accomplished their objective, the swindle of the Canal, and honesty and fairplay are meaningless.

Many people today accept the surrender of the Canal and the Panama Treaties as a fait accompli—but they do not have to—because the truth is forever recorded in The Panama Canal Treaties Swindle. Perhaps the truth is the most important thing of all!

Even at this hour, it is not too late to save some of the Panama bases to help protect American interests at the Isthmus of Panama. Calls and letters to the President and to senators and congressmen could make a difference.

The falsehoods and dishonesty that characterize the Panama Treaties bring to mind Thomas Paine's admonition during the Revolutionary War: "It is an affront to treat falsehood with complacency." Or, should the modern rule simply be "political correctness"?

The Panama Treaties for surrender of the Canal were several decades in formulating. They did not just happen overnight. There were definite milestones along the road to surrender from 1926 to 1974 and some of the most famous names in modern history should be forever etched in those milestones: President Franklin D. Roosevelt, Alger Hiss, Henry Kissinger, President Dwight D. Eisenhower, President John F. Kennedy and President Lyndon B. Johnson. There were ten milestones, Appendix G, and the Kissinger name goes on two of them: abrogation of the 1914 Bryan-Chammoro Treaty with Nicaragua, and the Kissinger-Tack Statement of Principles that incorrectly three times out of eight principles alleged that the Canal Zone was "Panamanian Territory." These Kissinger capitulations were extremely damaging to negotiations in the 1977 Panama Treaties.

This analysis of the swindle of the century should

definitely not omit the identities of the U.S. senators and representatives who voted to surrender the Canal. Appendix H is the Roll Call of the senators with notations about those soon defeated at elections. Appendix J is the Roll Call of the representatives who agreed to the implementation of the Treaties, thereby agreeing to surrender of the Canal and all supporting installations, 32 billion dollars worth of U.S. taxpayers' property. Representatives did not have to vote to implement the Treaties. Our constitutional system of checks and balances could have halted the surrender of the Canal at that point by the House of Representatives, who constitutionally could have refused to implement the Treaties. The vote was 232 to 188; so, 188 representatives refused surrender of the Canal.

National Security Center President Richard Delgaudio concurs. As an Account Executive at the direct mail agency, Bruce W. Eberle & Associates, Inc., he wrote fund appeals on this theme in 1978, signed by U.S. Senator Orrin Hatch aide Ronald F. Docksai, then Chairman of the Council for Inter-American Security. The letters said, "let's make this next election a referendum on the Panama Canal." The argument of the direct mail packets was that citizens should demand to know where their House of Representative candidates stood on the implementation of the Panama Canal Treaties before they decided who to vote for. Despite building Richard's client a powerful base of support, alas, that more of our citizens did not listen to this admonition in that year's election.

CHAPTER 9

Red China Gains A Foothold at the Panama Canal

This astonishing chapter title is accurate—hard to believe, but it happened. I first learned through confidential sources in the spring of 1997 that allies of Red China secured far-reaching "rights" and control over several key installations at the Panama Canal—including the Canal ports of Balboa and Cristobal.

Hutchison Whampoa—a Hong Kong business whose owner is an "allied consultant" to Communist China—won the contract to operate the ports at the Panama Canal. And these ports were turned over to this ally of Red China even though American and other companies gave better bids. This contract could eventually give Red China control over our Panama Canal when the U.S. withdraws in 1999.

Communist China is the greatest emerging threat to United States security. It has the largest army in the world, may soon have the second largest economy, and is rapidly building up its navy and air force. In fact, many scholars are sounding the alarm about a "new Cold War" with Red China, and a new book has just come out warning of a coming war with China.

Strategic spot for Red China

And now the Clinton Administration has allowed allies of Red China—the greatest threat to American national security—to take over the Canal ports and possibly secure other critical military facilities at the Panama Canal, only 900 miles from the United States!

The danger to the United States is very real. America will lose control of this vital choke-point, through which massive amounts of shipping and our U.S. Navy pass between the Pacific and Atlantic Oceans.

The ports of Balboa, which controls the shipping traffic from the Pacific Ocean, and Cristobal, which controls shipping from the Atlantic, will be run by Communist Chinese allies. The U.S. Navy could be denied access through the Canal ports, which have been critical to our military efforts in World War II, Korea, Vietnam, and the Persian Gulf conflicts.

Red Chinese J-11 attack jets, if launched from air facilities in Panama, could strike the mainland United States. Each J-11 can drop over 13,000 pounds of bombs—and China will have over 100 J-11's in the next few years. This is the potential should Red China muscle into U.S. air bases in Panama.

Communist China will also have a critical base for its warships in our backyard with the Balboa and Cristobal ports. Further, if Rodman Naval Station is handed over to Red China if the United States evacuates in 1999, it will give them a deep water port that can provide a base of operations for their warships and submarines only 900 miles from the United States.

But what is Bill Clinton doing about this dire threat to American national security? Nothing! He is standing by while allies of his Red Chinese campaign contributor friends take control of the vital Panama Canal ports!

Stunning developments at Panama Canal

How did such a stunning and disastrous series of events lead to allies of Communist China taking control of the Panama Canal ports, you may ask? The answer is, sadly, incompetence and possible corruption. Let's examine the following.

Hutchison Whampoa, Ltd. is a massive conglomerate based in Hong Kong. Its head, Li Ka-shing is one of the most powerful men in Hong Kong and has very close ties to the Communist Chinese government. (See section on Hutchison Whampoa, Ltd. ties to Red China, below) As I already reported, Hutchison Whampoa has been given control over the strategic ports of Balboa and Cristobal at each end of the Canal. But Hutchison Whampoa has also been given long term "options" for other facilities, including several military installations the United States is scheduled to evacuate.

Hutchison Whampoa was given this far-reaching deal by the Government of Panama, which was seeking the best money-making deal possible for themselves from the Canal and other U.S. properties.

So, without regard to the security of the Canal, their own country, or the United States, the Government of Panama entered into what amounts to a 50 year "contract" with Hutchison Whampoa, Ltd.—whose leader has close ties to Red China and whose home base, Hong Kong, is taken over by Communist China July 1, 1997.

This contract is spelled out in detail in the Government of Panama's Law No. 5, passed on January 16, 1997 by Panama's Legislative Assembly. Panama made its deal with Hutchison Whampoa without consultation with the United States, in some respects in violation of the 1977 Panama Canal Treaties and its own Constitution.

Who is Hutchison Whampoa?

Probably the most stunning recent development at the Panama Canal was the contract handing control of the strategic ports guarding each end of the Canal over to a company which is a key ally of Communist China. And this 50 year contract was only discovered in the United States after it was a done deal!

On March 1, 1997, Panama turned over the American-built piers and ports facilities at Balboa on the Pacific side and Cristobal on the Atlantic side in what appears to be a sharp break from American influence and toward a better money-making deal with Hutchison Whampoa.

Now, on the surface, Hutchison Whampoa, Ltd. appears to be a private, independent company from Hong Kong. But Hong Kong will be taken over by Red China by the time this book is published (July 1, 1997), and history has proven that when the communists move in, they do not tolerate anyone who does not toe the party line.

That does not appear to be a problem for Hutchison Whampoa, however. In fact, it appears that Hutchison Whampoa and its leader, Li Ka-shing, already have a very good understanding with Red China.

For example, Hutchison Whampoa is the only company that Communist China trusts to run its commercial ports, and is virtually running South China's seaborne trade. In fact, Hutchison Whampoa has been accused of having a "cozy relationship" with Red China that is as "close as lips and teeth".

Further, Li Ka-shing "is sure to be standing next to the top leaders of Beijing" in Red China when the Communist takeover occurs, according to a Journal of Commerce report by Joe Studwell. And Hong

Kong Congresswoman Emily Lau says the head of Hutchison Whampoa is already "a close advisor to the Chinese government".

Panama's Law No. 5 is a Shocker

Hutchison Whampoa and Panama negotiated Panama's Law No. 5 that would give them and their Communist Chinese allies a real foothold at the Panama Canal.

Law No. 5 was passed by Panama's Legislative Assembly on January 16, 1997 and published in the "Official Gazette" on January 21st, at which time it became law. A careful reading of this law should jolt our leaders in the State Department, the White House and the Congress. Of particular concern is the part which surrenders the strategic ports of Balboa and Cristobal. Indeed, it was a jolt for the members of the Merchant Marine Panel of the House Committee on National Security, including Chairman Herbert Bateman, R-Va., and ranking member Gene Taylor, D-Miss.

Law No. 5 is called a "contract" for operating the ports of Balboa and Cristobal, but it really is much more. It is also a long-term plan for shocking concessions and usurpation of unwarranted authority after the Americans depart on December 31, 1999 (the U.S. surrender date under the Panama Canal Treaties).

Who did the unorthodox negotiating which led to Law No. 5 and the usurpation of authority by allies of Communist China? It was Hugo Torrijos, nephew of the late dictator Omar Torrijos, the man who signed the Panama Canal Treaties without constitutional authority. Hugo's Panamanian negotiating partner was Minister of

Commerce Raul Casteazoro Arango, a member of one of the fourteen "ruling families" of Panama.

Negotiating for Hutchison Whampoa was the prestigious Panamanian Law firm of Morgan and Morgan. One of the Morgan partners is Eduardo Morgan, currently ambassador to the United States. Ambassador Morgan recently took umbrage in The Washington Times to a column of mine exposing the confusion in Panama in trying to "dispose" of the $32 billion worth of U.S. taxpayer property soon to drop in Panama's lap.

Secretive aspects of Law No. 5

Anyway, there are many aspects of Law No. 5 that are very secretive and very interesting:

• It received very little publicity, apparently because the Panamanian people are strongly anti-Communist and would react harshly to their government's handing over control of the ports to allies of Red China!

• Panama's leading newspaper La Prensa had virtually nothing to say on the matter. Publisher Roberto Eisenmann opposes any U.S. presence in Panama after 1999, so he didn't sound any alarms when Law No. 5 passed.

• TV Channel 4, owned by former Foreign Minister Fernando Eleta, was silent. Mr. Eleta also wants the Americans out!

• Law No. 5 is called a "Concessions and Investment Contract," but it is obviously more than just a business deal when it comes to operating the Panama Canal. In fact, Law No. 5 violates Article 274 of the Panamanian Constitution which requires a plebiscite on Panama Canal matters. None was held.

• Article 2.lld of Law No. 5 violates the guarantee

of "expedited treatment" of U.S. warships agreed to in Article VI and Amendment (2) of the Panama Neutrality Treaty by denying use of port facilities if such use would interfere with Hutchison Whampoa's operations.

• Hutchison Whampoa goes by the name of "Panama Ports Company" in Law No. 5, apparently a cover-up so the Panamanian people will not connect Hutchison with the Communist Chinese.

Can Panama ignore the Treaties?

Apparently, the Panamanian government feels that they can bypass portions of the Panama Canal Treaties that restrict their unfettered use of the Canal facilities profitable to them. Panama is a sovereign nation, it is true, but it agreed to the Treaties and is honor-bound to respect all portions of them, just as is the United States.

In the same vein, Panamanian President Ernesto "Toro" Balladares agreed with President Clinton on September 6th, 1995 in the Oval Office to hold exploratory talks for base rights negotiations. The talks never happened. Instead, President Balladares scoured Europe and Asia for money-making deals for the U.S. bases and other properties being surrendered in 1999.

President Balladares was reported "happy to sign" Law No. 5, even as Hong Kong—obviously under pressure from its soon-to-be master Red China—threatened to close the Panamanian consulate unless Panama broke diplomatic ties with Taiwan.

Red China at the Panama Canal:
A done deed?

On March 1, 1997 Hutchison Whampoa took over the American-built piers and ports at Balboa and Cristobal—to renovate and operate these strategic facilities at each end of the Canal. These are the piers and ports given to Panama in 1979 under terms of the 1977 Panama Treaties and allowed to deteriorate under Panamanian mismanagement. Now, Hutchison Whampoa and their Red Chinese friends can clean up the mess and, at the same time, occupy controlling spots at each end of the Canal as the Americans look on!

U.S. Ambassador to Panama William Hughes has pointed out that Hutchison Whampoa's bids for these ports—reportedly at $22.2 million each year—were "highly irregular". Two other companies (Bechtel and Kawasaki) reportedly gave better bids, giving credibility to the suspicion that Communist China may be in cahoots with the government of Panama for a better money-making deal for Panama's politicians and a better strategic position for Red China.

The U.S. Ambassador was kept in the dark on this highly irregular deal, too. He only received a copy of the Law four weeks after it had been adopted by the legislature—by a concerned American! So too was the Panama Canal Commission kept out of the loop. The Public Affairs Director there, Willie Friar, told me on March 14th, 1997 that she had "not heard" of this law—two weeks after it took effect!

So why did everyone work so hard to keep this deal quiet? Could it be that Hutchison Whampoa wanted to work as quietly as possible to secure the Panama Canal installations before anyone could stop them? It may be.

According to Aquilino Ortega Luna, writing in El Panama America for March 13th, 1997, Hutchison Whampoa is investing heavily in port modernization at Balboa and Cristobal preparing for the long haul—and well they might, for their contract runs for 50 years.

U.S.A. out, Red China In

Some of the shocking provisions of this hush-hush law, as it pertains to U.S. security, give Hutchison Whampoa and their Communist Chinese allies many "rights" that are potentially disastrous to America:

• Article 2.1 grants Hutchison Whampoa the option of controlling Diablo (town site) and Telfers Island, the latter a potential monitoring site for Galeta Island, the strategic U.S. communications station on the Atlantic side. With it the Communists could spy on us!

• Article 2.1 also allows a monopoly for Hutchison Whampoa against any competition at Diablo and Telfers Island.

• Article 2.1 further grants "first option" to Hutchison Whampoa to take over the superb U.S. Rodman Naval Station for use as a general commercial port. U.S. warships could be shut out, and Communist Chinese warships let in.

• Article 2.8 authorizes Hutchison Whampoa to "transfer contract rights" to any third party "registered" in Panama. This could be Iraq, Iran, Libya, or of course Communist China—bad news for a secure Canal.

• Article 2.10c grants Hutchison Whampoa the "right" to operate piloting services, tugs and work boats, inferring control of Canal pilots. In other words, Communist China could control the critical Canal pilots—and in turn, which ships go through the Canal and when—through their ally Hutchison Whampoa.

• Article 2.10e grants Hutchison Whampoa the "right" to control Diablo Road and Gaillard Avenue as private roads instead of public roads, thereby cutting off access to strategic areas of the Canal.

• Article 2.12a grants Hutchison Whampoa priority to all piers, including private piers, at Balboa and Cristobal, plus an operating area at Albrook Air Force Station. Will the Chinese J-11 attack aircraft use this operating area in the future?

• Article 2.12i guarantees Hutchison Whampoa the "right" to designate their own Canal pilots, change the rules for boarding vessels and add additional pilots—if clients claim dissatisfaction. One client who could claim dissatisfaction is, of course, Communist China.

Bill Bright Marine gave a briefing on this subject at a National Security Center breakfast at the Washington, DC Omni Shoreham Hotel during the Conservative Political Action Conference, introduced by NSC President Delgaudio. And, this information, at NSC's request, was shared on March 7th, 1997 to senior staff members of the following Senate Committees: Foreign Relations, Intelligence, and Armed Forces. In addition, it was provided to the office of Congressman Phil Crane, R-IL, who has long sought to save the Canal and some of the U.S. bases in Panama. None had seen Law No. 5 and all were surprised and very interested. We are indebted to Bill Bright Marine for his service in helping get the word out about this startling development.

Red China gives money to Panamanians too—
not just President Clinton

Why would Panamanian authorities agree to such far-reaching concessions, given the vital strategic importance of this choke-point? Congressman Leopoldo Bennedetti of the Panamanian Legislative Assembly may have the answer, as quoted in El Siglo recently: "Bucket loads of money from Asian contractors are pouring in." Added another legislator: "The government is receiving 'money under the table' for public bids that favor the Asians."

American companies, bidding on the up-and-up, have been shut out of business opportunities in Panama, prompting Ambassador Hughes to send a letter of protest to Minister of Commerce Raul Gasteazoro Arango about the "unfair treatment in Panama". However, Minister Arango is the man who negotiated the lopsided Law No. 5 in the first place, so his protest fell on deaf ears. Among the American companies discriminated against are: Varian Associates, Unisys, Saybolt, The Ports, Manzanillo International Terminal, Kansas City Southern Railway and Cellular Vision.

Consent to Disaster

The subtitle of my previous book The Panama Canal Treaties Swindle is Consent to Disaster. Is this subtitle becoming prophetic as the Americans prepare to move out and the Communist Chinese prepare to move in?

Adding to the potential for disaster is the apparently secretive 1996 State-of-the-Canal study by the U.S.

Army Corps of Engineers, reporting the Canal's "lack of maintenance". After being provided an "unofficial" copy of the overview of this study by National Security Center, I attempted to obtain an "official" copy from the Panama Canal Commission but was told it was too "political" and "sensitive."

The study was then reprinted and distributed in the United States by the non-profit National Security Center. This study shows that it has been known to both our Government and the Government of Panama that the Canal is deteriorating and will become inoperable unless the necessary and long overdue maintenance is conducted.

Now, with Communist China expanding its foothold at the Canal and with this long overdue and neglected maintenance to boot, can we be hearing the death knell of the Panama Canal, as we have known it?

In fact, that is why the title of this book is Death Knell of the Panama Canal?. From the very moment that Jimmy Carter gave away this Wonder of the World that we Americans built and paid for, I have been warning about the pending disaster that handing the Panama Canal over to the Government of Panama would be. I have documented over the years the deterioration of the Panama Canal and its facilities, under PCC control, and warned of the consequences of evacuating the Panama Canal bases in 1999.

Both nations grossly at fault

And, of course, I have researched and updated the far-reaching implications of the Government of Panama's Law No. 5 that has opened the door for Communist China at the Isthmus of Panama and a foothold at our Panama Canal.

In their zeal to reap the financial benefits from this deal, the Government of Panama has thrown caution and security to the wind. Worse, they have disregarded the Panama Neutrality Treaty giving United States vessels "expeditious passage" through the Canal and their own Constitution which requires a plebiscite on Canal matters.

Now, we might have predicted (and we have) that the corruption and greed in the Panamanian Government would endanger the security and operations at the Panama Canal. But what we could not have predicted is the complete lack of interest in the United States government to protect its national security and Treaty rights.

There is a disturbing neglect of security matters in the Clinton Administration, in refusing to move to protect our clear and vital interests in Panama and in refusing to assert American rights spelled out in the Panama Treaties.

We can only hope that Congress, now aware of the dire situation the Panamanian Government and the Clinton Administration have led us to, will act immediately to halt the Communist Chinese infiltration into the Panama Canal and re-assert American security interests at this vital waterway.

This lack of interest in the Panama Canal has been evident also at the Conservative Political Action Conference, which National Security Center stopped co-sponsoring several years ago after its unwillingness to officially sanction a panel discussion of this issue. Hence the origin of the NSC annual briefing at the site of CPAC. CPAC delegates who attend our annual briefing must skip a regular CPAC panel, usually on Saturday morning every year.

One year when NSC's arguments to have an official

CPAC Panama Canal panel were being shot down by the other co-sponsors, it was noted that no less than three other organizations' fundraising appeals were circulating in the mail, saying the "giveaway of the Panama Canal should be stopped." Another year I was asked to address this matter to a co-sponsors breakfast planning meeting. To no avail.

And yet the Panama Canal continues to be a topic of interest to many, whose continuing support enables National Security Center's work to go on each year.

Some closing thoughts

In these pages we have reported on some of the details that can definitely doom this great waterway and Wonder of the World—the Panama Canal, a world-famous monument to American ingenuity and generosity, now about to be shamefully surrendered because of a timid U.S. president who placed appeasement and popularity above the security and honor of his own country: Jimmy Carter, who, many have said, would have served America better by sticking to peanuts.

Let us not forget the presidents who followed Carter and who had the golden opportunity to right this wrong and keep campaign promises to boot: Ronald Reagan and George Bush, both of whom had told voters of the importance of holding onto the Canal, but who, once in office, had been supplied with books and documentation to prove illegal Treaties but declined to move a muscle!

As for Democratic President Bill Clinton, one wonders how much he ever knew about the Canal or truly, if he cared about it. He was reported to have spent "less than an hour" on the Canal issue in his four years in office. His record shows that he was quite busy doing whatever it takes to get reelected.

Three major developments are threatening the future of Canal operations, as we have known them, and may be precursors of the very death knell of this great maritime gateway:

• When the Canal operators, the Panama Canal Commission, allow this 83-year old treasure to deteriorate because of "lack of maintenance caused by the need to lock ships" for more Canal tolls, something is wrong.

• When the Government of Panama, soon to be sole operator of the Canal, turns over strategic ports at each end of the Canal to allies of Communist China, who calls the USA "our main enemy", and enters into a 50-year lease undermining the very future of the Canal, something is wrong.

• When the Government of the United States, under a president and State Department oblivious to U.S. rights and interests at the Isthmus of Panama, condones unconstitutional Treaties and incursions against Treaty rights, and makes virtually no effort in 19 years to preserve U.S. interests at the Canal, something is wrong.

Obviously, the Panama Canal Commission neglected Canal maintenance too long and now has on its hands an embarrassing State-of-the-Canal report by the U.S. Army Engineers that they had to classify "politically sensitive", while scrambling to save the Canal.

The Panamanian Government, still under one of the fourteen ruling families since its birth in 1903 and still having big bucks as a top priority, is welcoming Communist China to a foothold at the Canal with potential in its Law No. 5 for future controls devastating to U.S. interests.

Communist China, in Party documents, classifies

the United States as "our main enemy". Panama's President Balladares does not care about this. He wants big dough for his big prize, the Canal and environs, and the Gringos can go to Blue Blazes! Canal security and any accommodation for the Americans seem furthest from his mind.

Balladares proved his contempt when he deceived President Clinton about holding "talks" for U.S. base rights. Instead, he procrastinated and skipped off to Europe and Asia for more money. He hit pay dirt with Red China, a developing maritime power, and was "happy to sign" Law No. 5 that turned over the Canal's controlling ports of Balboa and Cristobal and that "granted" extensive "rights" to an enemy of the United States.

Indeed, the handwriting is on the wall: In a few short years, Communist China could become the Canal operator, and U.S. warships needing "expeditious passage", as guaranteed by the Panama Treaties, could just wait their turns. Will Americans stand for this?

Red China as Canal boss

In future years, Panama, despite the professional training given its engineers by the departing Gringos, could become incompetent for the long haul and could welcome the Red Chinese to come to the rescue as Canal boss and operator. Time will tell, but little is rosy for the USA as the year 1999 approaches.

The U.S. government, under Presidents Reagan, Bush and Clinton and under political leaders Dole, Lott and Gingrich, have largely ignored citizens' concerns about the surrender of the Canal by illegal Treaties and the urgent need to negotiate for U.S. base rights.

Moreover, many Americans seem to accept loss of

this great asset as a fait accompli. They have other things to do and after all, time fades memories. Besides, our major media have not reported the swindle story, have not updated developments, but have, in most cases, taken the side of "Justice for Panama", i.e., surrender the Canal and forget base rights!

If our words are harsh—about the Panama Canal Commission, Panamanian President Balladares, U.S. Presidents Reagan, Bush and Clinton, the ruling elite of Panama and other U.S. leaders—they are considered necessary as an unadulterated approach to a harsh problem: the swindle of 32 billion dollars worth of U.S. taxpayers' property under false pretenses by elected leaders who, even today, refuse to remedy this travesty. The issue involves security of our country—indeed, our national honor.

Things left to do

This author has worked thousands of hours, traveled thousands of miles, spoken hundreds of times and written volumes of essays and two books on the injustice of the 1977 Panama Canal Treaties and the shame our leaders inflict on us for not standing up for our rights and "Justice for America." Sadly, our statesmen are too busy being "politically correct" in the New World Order—and getting reelected! They have not taken the time to discover the crude manipulations of the Carter Administration in producing these Treaties, despite being handed a personal copy of the 424 page exposure, The Panama Canal Treaties Swindle: Consent to Disaster (Signal Books).

This is my second book about the hypocrisy and shame of the Canal swindle and the betrayal of American voters by President Carter in his naïve effort to do good, after having solemnly promised "never to give up control of the Panama Canal"—adding, "I'll never lie to you!"

Those readers who have come with us this far have a great deal of information and it is accurate. No major points in my books and essays have ever been disproved.

These readers have to believe that they and their concerns are important, but only if they make them known to their two senators and congressman. Tell them politely and firmly:

• We must not surrender the Panama Canal with illegal Treaties.

• We must renegotiate the Panama Treaties to provide a U.S.-Panama partnership to operate the Canal.

• We must negotiate at once for U.S. base rights in Panama to include Howard Air Force Base, Rodman Naval Station, Fort Sherman, Galeta Island and Quarry Heights Headquarters of the U.S. Southern Command.

• We must notify Panama that operation of the strategic ports of Balboa and Cristobal by an ally of Communist China is unacceptable and an infringement on U.S. rights under the 1977 Panama Canal Treaties.

Strong beliefs and determination will be needed to stir our Washington leaders out of their preoccupation with self-aggrandizement and getting reelected—and to get them to focus on the disaster looming 900 miles south of our borders. Follow-ups and more and more follow-ups are usually required to get decent responses from our congressional leaders whose staffs routinely use form letters that do not address our inquiry at all. That's where patience and determination come into play. But, that's the way of life in Washington, and that has been my experience many times—overcome only by persistence. Perhaps we need congressional staffs sensitive to reality.

We title our book, Death Knell of the Panama Canal?—with a question mark—a pretty good title when we consider all that now threatens the Canal and that could bring on the death knell of what once was, and still should be, the Pride of America!

We can still try to save our Canal. We must try! The stirring words of Teddy Roosevelt, our 26th president and a man not afraid of the devil, are very appropriate for our endeavors at this time. President Roosevelt told his critics and detractors just what was on his mind—and he minced no words:

It is not the critic who counts— nor the man who points out how the strong man stumbled or how the doer of deeds should have done better. The credit belongs to the man in the arena whose face is covered with blood and sweat and dirt—and who, if he fails, at least fails while doing greatly—so that his place shall never be with those cold, timid souls who know neither victory not defeat.

A final word: Let's do it!

APPENDIX A

Panama's Counter-Reservation to the Panama Canal Treaties

The Republic of Panama agrees to the exchange of the instruments of ratification of the aforementioned Neutrality Treaty on the understanding that there are positive rules of international law contained in multilateral treaties to which both the Republic of Panama and the United States of America are Parties and which consequently both States are bound to implement in good faith, such as Article 1, paragraph 2 and Article 2, paragraph 4 of the Charter of the United Nations, and Article 18 and 20 of the Charter of the Organization of American States.

It is also the understanding of the Republic of Panama that the actions which either party may take in exercise of its rights and the fulfillment of its duties in accordance with the aforesaid Treaty, including measures to reopen the canal and to restore its normal operation, if it should be interrupted or obstructed, will be effected in a manner consistent with the principles of mutual respect and cooperation on which the new relationship established by that Treaty is based.

The Republic of Panama declares that its political independence, territorial integrity and self-determination are guaranteed by the unshakeable will of the Panamanian people. Therefore, the Republic of Panama will reject, in unity and with decisiveness and firmness, any attempt by any country to intervene in its internal or external affairs. (Emphasis added)

NOTE: Panama's counter-reservation was contained in Panama's Instrument of Ratification to the Panama Canal Treaty and in Panama's Instrument of Ratification to the Neutrality Treaty—but not in the United States instruments, as customary and required. Hence, there are two versions of the Treaties. This major change, requiring Panama's "cooperation" for any U.S. defense of the Canal, was never voted on by the U.S. Senate, a violation of Article II of the U.S. Constitution. A survey in 1982 proved that eight senators would have voted "NO" if they had seen this counter-reservation and the Treaties would have failed.

APPENDIX B

December 14, 1994

Mr. Richard A. Delgaudio
President, National Security Center
3554 Chain Bridge Rd., Suite 301
Fairfax, VA 22030

Dear Mr. Delgaudio:

I shall not delay another moment in thanking you and the National Security Center for so effectively educating both the general public and Senators about the background and activities of Mr. Robert Pastor, the controversial Clinton nominee to be U.S. Ambassador to Panama.

As the National Security Center documented, Pastor presided over one of the most humiliating periods in the history of U.S. foreign policy in Latin America. My own review of formerly classified documents raised additional serious concerns that Pastor may have been in violation of the law in seeking foreign aid in 1980 for the communist Sandinistas. Pastor's record clearly disclosed that he certainly did not deserve to be rewarded with an Ambassadorship.

The thousands of concerned citizens who signed petitions opposing the Pastor nomination proved again that the American people have not forgotten the shameful undermining of U.S. interests during the Carter Administration. In organizing the petition effort, the National Security Center made a valuable contribution in our efforts to prevent President Clinton from sending this controversial nominee to Panama. I personally and genuinely appreciate the National Security Center's help in making known the Pastor record.

God bless you, and best wishes for a joyful and meaningful Holy Season.

Sincerely,

JESSE HELMS
U.S. Senator

APPENDIX C

Schedule of U.S. Property Transfers

(under the Panama Canal Treaty Implementation Plan—February 1995)
U.S. Southern Command
Transferred through 1994: 420 buildings, 16,600 acres: 17% of total
To be transferred by 2000: 4,200 buildings, 77,000 acres: 83% of total

1993 transfers
1 Jul—Camp Chagres Area
1 Sep—Chiva Chiva Range

1994 transfers
31 May—Coco Solo Health Clinic
31 May—Summit Radio site

1995 transfers
30 Jun—Margarita Schl Bldg
1 Aug—Cristobal High School
1 Sep—Fort Espinar
15 Sep—Mindi Vet Clinic
15 Sep—Fort Davis

1996 transfers
31 Jan—Fort Amador
1 Jul—Curundu High School
30 Sep—Curundu Flats

1997 transfers
1 Jul—Diablo Elem School
1 Oct—Albrook AF Station

1998 transfers
1 Apr—Gorgas Hospital
1 Apr—Herrick Heights
1 Aug—Panama Canal College
1 Aug—Los Rios Elem School
1 Oct—Quarry Heights
1 Oct—Morgan Avenue

1999 transfers
Fort Kobbe
Cocoli
Corozal Army Base
Curundu Laundry
Cerro Gordo Comm.
Bldg 1501—Balboa
Fort Sherman
Pina Training Center
Chiva Chiva
Balboa Elem School
Balboa High School
Ancon Hill Comm.
Fort Clayton
Fort Davis
Ammo Supply Point #1
Empire Range
Howard Air Force Base
Semaphore Hill
Balboa West Range
Rodman Naval Station
Farfan
Arraijan Tank Farm
Marine Corps Barracks
Galeta Island
Margarita

A total of 46 U.S. properties are scheduled for transfer to Panama and, added to the Canal and its facilities, are valued at $32 billion worth of U.S. taxpayers investments.

Troop reduction from 9,000 to 7,000 by the end of 1995 is scheduled. Military families will be reduced by 2,000 by the end of 1995.

APPENDIX D

Milestones to Surrender

Originally, the Panamanians were happy with the 1903 Treaty: independence was guaranteed; $10 million in gold; malaria and yellow fever controlled; jobs and the economy better. But it did not take long to prove the Latin American axiom: "The more one shakes the Yankee tree, the more plums one gathers." Milestones mark the road to the proposed surrender of $32 billion worth of Yankee taxpayers' property:

Milestone No. 1 was the proposed 1926 Treaty which, although never ratified, would soften treaty enforcement. It signified a shift by the U.S. from the "big stick" to "good neighbor."

Milestone No. 2 was the 1936 Hull-Alfaro Treaty, an outgrowth of President Franklin Roosevelt's "Good Neighbor Policy," featuring generous aid, 14 major concessions, including sharing Canal defense with Panama.

Milestone No. 3 was the surrender of defense base rights in 1942 to be effective one year after World War II.

Milestone No. 4 was the unauthorized listing in 1946 of the Canal Zone as "occupied territory" by Alger Hiss in his United Nations Report.

Milestone No. 5 was the 1955 Chapin-Fabrega Treaty with more concessions, including increased annuity to almost $2 million and voiding U.S. rights to regulate sanitation in Colon and Panama City, among others.

Milestone No. 6 was President Dwight Eisenhower's capitulation in 1960 to permit Panama's flag alongside the U.S. flag in Shaler's Triangle in the Canal Zone as evidence of "titular sovereignty"—a costly mistake that signaled the beginning of the end.

Milestone No. 7 was President John Kennedy's error in 1963 permitting Panama's flag to be flown in the Canal Zone everywhere the U.S. flag flew, thereby compounding Eisenhower's mistake. Flags signify sovereignty, historically and universally; therefore, these orders of Presidents Eisenhower and Kennedy were contrary to the 1903 Treaty granting U.S. sovereign rights, "to the entire exclusion" of any Panamanian sovereign rights. At best, they signified weakness.

Milestone No. 8 was President Lyndon Johnson's capitulation in 1964 to renegotiate the 1903 Treaty and to surrender sovereign rights, thereby weakening future U.S. negotiating positions.

Milestone No. 9 was the needless abrogation in 1971 of the 1914 Bryan-Chammoro Treaty with Nicaragua, thereby surrendering U.S. rights for a canal through Nicaragua, plus 99 year leases on the Corn Island in the Caribbean and base rights on the Gulf of Fonseca—all initiated by Secretary of State Henry Kissinger.

Milestone No. 10 marked another error by Kissinger: The Kissinger-Tack Statement of Principles in 1974 incorrectly alleging three times out of eight principles that the Canal Zone is "Panamanian territory"—totally contrary to rulings of the U.S. Supreme Court in 1907 and the 5th Circuit Court of Appeals in 1971. These erroneous "Principles" became the basis for the 1977 Treaties, and Kissinger became "the Architect of the 1977 Panama Treaties."

APPENDIX E

Senators Voting to Surrender the Panama Canal on April 18, 1978

John Sparkman, D-Ala.***James Culver, D-Iowa*
Mike Gravel, D-Alas.*James Pearson, R-Kan.*
Dennis DeConcini, D-Ariz.W. Huddleston, D-Kan.**
Dale Bumpers, D-Ark.Russell Long, D-La.
Kaneaster Hodges, D-Ark.**William Hathaway, D-Me.*
Alan Cranston, D-Cal.Edwin Muskie, D-Me.***
S.I. Hayakawa, R-Cal.***Charles Mathias, R-Md.
Gary Hart, D-Colo.Paul Sarbanes, D-Md.
Foyd Haskell, D-Colo.*Edward Brooke, R-Mass.*
Abraham Ribicoff, D-Conn.***Edward Kennedy, D-Mass.
Lowell Weicker, R-Conn.Donald Riegle, D-Mich.
Joseph Biden, D-Del.W. Anderson, D-Minn.*
Lawton Chiles, D-Fla.Muriel Humphrey, D-Minn.**
Richard Stone, D-Fla.*John Danforth, R-Mo.
Sam Nunn, D-Ga.T. Eagleston, D-Mo.
Herman Talmadge, D-Ga.*Paul Hatfield, D-Mont.***
Daniel Inouye, D-Haw.Howard Cannon, D-Nev.*
Spark Matsunaga, D-Haw.John Durkin, D-N.H.*
Frank Church, D-Ida.*T. McIntyre, D-N.H.*
Charles H. Percy, R-Ill.**C. P. Case, R-N.J.**
Adlai Stevenson, D-Ill.*H. Williams, D-N.J.***
Birch Bayh, D- Ind.*Jacob Javits, R-N.Y.***
Dick Clark, D-Iowa*Daniel Moynihan, D-N.Y.
John Glenn, D-OhioGeorge McGovern, D-S.D.**
 H. Metzenbaum, D-OhioHoward Baker, R-Tenn.***
Henry Bellmon, R-Okla.James Sasser, D-Tenn.
M. O. Hatfield, R-Ore.Lloyd Bentsen, D-Tex.
R. Packwood, R-Ore.Patrick Leahy, D-Ver.
Robert Morgan, D-N.C.*Robert Stafford, R-Ver.
John Heinz, R-Pa.Henry Jackson, D-Wash.***
John Chafee, R-R.I.W. Magnuson, D-Wash.*
Claiborne Pell, D-R.I.Robert Byrd, D-W.Va.
Ernest Hollings, D-S.C.Gaylord Nelson, D-Wis.***
James Abourezk, D-S.D.William Proxmire, D-Wis.

* Defeated in general election ** Defeated in primary election ***
Retired or resigned

NOTE: 35 of these Senators who voted to surrender the Panama
Canal were no longer in the Senate after next elections: many attributed
their defeat to their votes on the Canal Treaties. In 1978, 10 were defeated
in the general election, 2 in the primary, and 4 retired. In 1980, 9 were defeated in the general election and 4 retired. In 1982, one was defeated,
Howard W. Cannon, D-Nev. In 1984, two were defeated, two retired and
one died.

The same 68 Senators listed above also consented to the Neutrality
Treaty on March 16, 1978.

APPENDIX F

Representatives Voting to Implement the Panama Canal Treaties on September 26, 1979

The following members of the U.S. House of Representatives voted to implement the Panama Canal Treaties (1977). The vote count was decisive, 232 to 188 with 196 Democrats and 36 Republicans agreeing to the Panama Canal Act of 1979 which became the second step required for the "surrender" of the Canal. The Canal could have been "saved" at that time by a House veto to reject the implementing legislation. In no way was approval mandatory. This was an important part of the Constitution's unique system of checks and balances. Did the peoples' representatives know this?

Democrats (196)

Joseph Addabbo, N.Y.Davis Bowen, Miss.†
Daniel Akaka, HawaiiJohn Brademas, Ind.†
Donald Albosta, Mich.John Breau, La.‡
Bill Alexander, Ark.Jake Brinkley, Ga.†‡
Jerome Ambro, N.Y.†WilliamBrodhead, Mic.†
Ike Andrews, N.C.Jack Brooks, Tex.
Frank Annuzio, Ill.George Brown, Cal.
Thomas Ashley, OhioBill Bulison, Mo.†
Les Aspin, Wisc.John Burton, Cal.†
Les AuCoin, Ore.Phillip Burton, Cal.
Alvin Baldus, Wisc.†Bob Carr, Mich.
Michael Barnes, Md.John Cavanaugh, Neb.†
Berkely Bedell, IowaShirley Chisholm, N.Y.†
Anthony Beilenson, Cal.†William Clay, Mo.
Adam Benjamin, Ind.Tony Coelho, Cal.
Mario Biaggi, N.Y.Cardiss Collins, Ill.
Jonathan Bingham, N.Y.†John Conyers, Mich.
James Blanchard, Mich.†James Corman, Cal.†
Corinne Boggs, La.‡William Cotter, Conn.†
Edward Boland, Mass.Norman D'Amours, NH†
Richard Bolling, Mo.†George Danielson, Cal.†

William Boner, Tenn.Thomas Daschle, S.D.
David Bonior, Mich.Mendel Davis, S.C.†
Don Bonker, Wash.Ronald Dellums, Cal.
Marilyn Bouquard, Tenn.‡Butler Derrick, S.C.
Norman Dicks, Wash.Kenneth Holland, S.C.†
Charles Diggs, Mich.†James Howard, N.J.
John Dingell, Mich.William Hughes, N.J.
Julian Dixon, Cal.Andrew Jacobs, Ind.‡
Christopher Dodd, Conn.†Edgar Jenkins, Ga.
Thomas Downey, N.Y.Ed Jones, Tenn.
Robert Drinan, Mass.James Jones, Okla.‡
Joseph Early, Mass.Robert Kastenmeier, WI
Robert Edgar, Pa.Dale Kildee, Mich.
Don Edwards, Cal.Raymond Kogovsek, CO.
Allen Ertel, Pa.†Peter Kostmayer, Pa.
Billy Lee Evans, Ga.†John La Falce, N.Y.
David Evans, Ind.†‡Raymond Lederer, Pa.†
John Fary, Ill.†William Lehman, Fla.
Dante Fascell, Fla.Mickey Leland, Tex.
Vic Fazio, Cal.Elliott Levitas, Ga.
Geraldine Ferraro, N.Y.†‡Clarence Long, Md.†
Joseph Fisher, Va.†Mike Lowry, Wash.
Floyd Fithian, Ind.†Stanley Lundine, N.Y.
James Florio, N.J.Mike McCormack, WA.†
Thomas Foley, Wash.Matthew McHugh, N.Y.
Harold Ford, Tenn.Gunn McKay, Utah†
William Ford, Mich.Andrew Maguire, N.J.†
Wyche Fowler, Jr., Ga.Edward Markey, Mass.
James Frost, Tex.†Robert Matsui, Cal.
Robert Garcia, N.Y.Nicholas Mavroules, Mas.
Richard Gephardt, Mo.Romano Mazzoli, Ky.
Robert Giaimo, CN†Daniel Mica, Fla.‡
Sam Gibbons, FL.Barbara Mikulski, Md.
Don Glickman, Kan.Abner Mikva, Ill.†
Henry Gonzalez, TXGeorge Miller, Cal.
Albert Gore, TN†Norman Mineta, Cal.
William Gray, PAJoseph Minish, N.J.
Frank Guarini, NJ‡Parren Mitchell, Md.
Tony Hall, OH†John Moakly, Mass.
Lee Hamilton, INToby Moffett, Conn.
Tom Harkin, Iowa†Robert Mollohan, W. Va.
Herbert Harris II, Va.†William Morehead, Pa.†

Augustus Hawkins, Cal.Austin Murphy, Pa.‡
Bill Hefner, NCJohn Murphy, N.Y.†
Cecil Hefnel, HA†John Murtha, Pa.
Michael Myers, PA†Neal Smith, Iowa
Stephen Neal, NCStephen Solarz, N.Y.
Lucien Nedzi, Mich.†Gladys Spellman, Md.†
Richard Nolan, Minn.†Fernand St. Germain, R.I.
Henry Nowak, NYEdward Stack, Fla.†
James Oberstar, Minn.Fortney Stark, Cal.
David Obey, Wisc.Tom Steed, Okla.†
Richard Ottinger, NYBennett Stewart, Ill.†
Leon Panetta, CALouis Stokes, Ohio
Edward Patten, CA†Gerry Studds, Mass.
Jerry Patterson, CAAl Swift, Wash.
Donald Pease, OHMichael Syndar, Okla.
Claude Pepper, FLFrank Thompson, Jr., NJ†
Peter Peyser, N.Y.†Bob Traxler, Mich.
Jake Pickle, Tex.Morris Udall, Ariz.
Richardson Preyer, N.C.†Al Ullman, Ore.†
Melvin Price, Ill.Lionell VanDeerlin, CA†
Charles Rangel, N.Y.Charles Vanik, OH†
William Ratchford, Conn.Bruce Vento, Minn.
Henry Reuss, Wisc.†Doug Walgren, Penn.
Frederick Richmond, N.Y.†Henry Waxman, Cal.
Robert Roe, N.J.James Weaver, Ore.
Dan Rostenkowski, Ill.Theodore Weiss, N.Y.
Edward Roybal, Cal.Charles H. Wilson, Cal.†
Marty Russo, Ill.Timothy Wirth, Colo.
Martin Sabo, Minn.Lester Wolff, N.Y.†
James Scheuer, N.Y.Howard Wolpe, Mich.
Patricia Schroeder, Colo.Jim Wright, Tex.
John Seiberling, OhioSidney Yates, Ill.
James Shannon, Mass.Robert Young, Mo.
Philip Sharp, Ind.Clement Zablocki, Wisc.
Paul Simon, Ill.Leo Zaferetti, N.Y.†

Republicans (36)
John Anderson, Ill.†James Jeffords, Ver.‡
Robin Beard, Tenn.†‡James Johnson, Colo.†
Douglas Bereuter, Neb.‡Jim Leach, Iowa
Ed Bethune, Ark.†‡Robert McClory, Ill.†‡
William Broomfield, Mich.Paul McCloskey, Cal.†

John Buchanan, Ala.†Stewart McKinney, Con.
Caldwell Butler, Va.†Marc Marks, Penn.†
Barber Conable, N.Y.†Charles Pashayan, Cal.‡
Silvio Conte, Mass.Joel Pritchard, Wash.
Edward Derwinski, Ill.†Carl Pursell, Mich.
John Erlenborn, Ill.Thomas Railsback, Ill.†
Millicent Fenwick, N.J.†John Rhodes, Ariz.†‡
Paul Findley, Ill.†Bill Royer, Cal.†‡
Hamilton Fish, Jr., N.Y.‡Harold Sawyer, Mich.‡
Edwin Forsythe, N.J.‡William Stanton, Ohio†
Bill Frenzel, Minn.David Stockman, Mich.†
William Green, N.Y.Bob Wilson, Cal.†
Harold Hollenbeck, N.J.†‡John Wydler, N.Y.†‡

† No longer in the House after the 1986 elections
‡ These 25 Congressmen voted on September 20, 1979 to reject the Conference Report of the Panama Canal Act of 1979, the implementing legislation, but switched their positions for the final vote on September 26, 1979 after minor changes had been made and following intensive lobbying by the White House and comments by Congressman Robert Bauman, R-Md.

Congressman Bauman, later discredited for shameful homosexual conduct, was apparently able to sway 13 of the 25 Republican Congressmen to switch their votes.

Frank Turberville, Jr. of the Canal Watchers' Educational Association sent separate letters to each of these 25 Congressmen asking what caused them to switch their positions. No answer from anyone was received.

BIBLIOGRAPHY

Brzezinski, Zbigniew. Power and Principle: Memoirs of the National Security Adviser, 1977-1981. New York: Farrar, Straus, Giroux, 1983.

Carter, Jimmy. Keeping Faith. New York: Bantam Books, 1982.

The Constitution of the United States of America

DuVal, Miles P., Jr. And the Mountains Will Move: The Story of the Building of the Panama Canal. Westport, Conn. Greenwood Press, 1968.

Cadiz to Cathay: The Story of the Long Kiplomatic Strucggle for the Panama Canal. Palo Alto, California: Stanford University Press, 1947.

"Isthmian Canal Policy—An Evaluation," U.S. Naval Institute Proceedings, vol. 81, no. 3, March 1995.

Evans, G. Russell. The Panama Canal Treaties Swindle: Consent to Disaster. Carrboro, North Carolina: Signal Books, 1986.

Flood, Daniel J. Isthmian Canal Policy Questions (House Document No. 474, 89th Congress). Washington: Government Printing Office, 1966.

Johnson, Lyndon B. The Vantage Point. New York: Holt, Reinhart & Winston, 1971.

Jorden, William J. Panama Odyssey. Austin, Texas: University of Texas Press, 1984.

Lane, Thomas A. The Breakdown of the Old Politics. New Rochelle, New York: Arlington House Publishers, 1974.

McCullough, David. The Path Between the Seas. New York: Simon and Schuster, 1977.

Norton, Thomas James. The Constitution of the United States: Its Sources and Application. New York: The World Publishing Company, 1943.

Stoll, Samuel J. Canalgate. Livingston, New Jersey: Policy Press, 1989.

U.S. Government
U.S. Senate

Implementing the Panama Canal Treaty of 1977 and Related Agreements. Senate Report No. 96-255, 96th Congress, 1st sess., July 21, 1979. Washington: U.S. Governent Printing Office, 1979.

Senate Debate of the Panama Canal Treaties, A compendium of Major Statements, Documents, Record Votes and Relevant Events. Washington: U.S. Government Printing Office, February 1979.

Panama Canal Treaties—Constitutional and Legal Aspects of the Ratification Process. Hearing before the Subcommittee on Separation of Powers of the Senate Committee on the Judiciary, 98th Congress, 1st sess., June 23, 1983. Washington: U.S. Government Printing Office, 1983.

The Panama Canal Treaty and the Congressional Power to Dispose of United States Property. Report to the Committee on the Judiciary made by its Subcommittee on Separation of Powers, 95th Congress, 2nd sess., February 1978. Washington: U.S. Government Printing Office, 1978.

U.S. House of Representatives

Constitution, Jefferson's Manual and Rules of the House of Representatives. House Document No. 95-403, 95th Congress, 2nd sess., William Holmes Brown, Parliamentarian. Washington: U.S. Government Printing Office, 1979.

U.S. Department of State

Documents Associated with the Panama Canal Treaties. Department of State Selected Documents, No. 6B, September 1977. Washington: U.S. Government Printing Office, 1977.

Texts of Treaties Relating to the Panama Canal. Department of State Selected Documents, No. 6A, September 1977. Washington: U.S. Government Printing Office, 1977.

Panama Canal Permanent Neutrality and Operations Treaty between the United States of America and Panama. Treaties and Other International Acts Series No. 10029, U.S. Department of State, signed at Washington, DC, September 7, 1977. Washington: U.S. Government Printing Office, 1982.

Panama Canal Treaty between the United States of America and Panama. Treaties and Other International Acts Series No. 10030, U.S. Department of State, Signed in Washington, DC, September 7, 1997. Washington: U.S. Government Printing Office, 1982.

Assessment of the Panama Canal, Treaties, No. 6A., Bureau of Public Affairs, U.S. Department of State. July 15, 1995.

Media

El Panama America, Panamanian newspaper.
El Siglo, Panamanian newspaper.
La Estrella de Panama, Panamanian newspaper.
La Prensa, Panamanian newspaper.
The Panama Canal Spillway, official newspaper of the Panama Canal Commission.
Time magazine.
The Washington Post, U.S. newspaper.
The Washington Times, U.S. newspaper.

Miscellaneous

Atlantic Council of the United States. Defining a New Relationship: The Issue of U.S. Access to Facilities in Panama. July 1996. Washington, DC.

Fellowship of Reconciliation Task Force on Latin America & the Caribbean. Panama Update. Autumn 1996.

General Accounting Office. Panama: DoD's Drawdown Plan for the U.s. Military in Panama. August 1995.

Hatheway, Gina Marie L., Professional Staff Member for Inter-American Affairs, U.S. Senate Foreign Relations Committee. Staff report on Base Rights negotiations with Panama. February 13, 1997.

Panama Canal Commission. Proposal to Increase Tolls and Apply Certain Rules. August 1996.

The Conservative Caucus. Defending the Panama Canal After 1999: What Role Will the United States Play? March 1995.

How you can help

The big book distributors told us no one's interested in the Panama Canal topic. So we self published *Death Knell of the Panama Canal?* by Captain G. Russell Evans and *Peril in Panama* by Richard A. Delgaudio. Thanks to our supporters and many concerned Americans we've distributed 447,000 copies of both books.

For both books, National Security Center relies on friends and concerned Americans to help us continue this work. Captain Evans' participation in three "Missions to Panama" and Richard Delgaudio's leading two additional fact-finding "Missions to Panama" are all paid for by voluntary donations. NSC newsletters and other publications are paid for by individual donors.

I urge you to consider a donation to help this work continue. Consider the author of this book or *Peril in Panama* as a speaker or help him get on the radio or a TV talk show. The year 1999 is the final year before U.S. troops are withdrawn and the last bases closed in Panama. It is urgent.

If you read about this book in a non-mainstream publication which relies upon individual donations to continue, please support them by sending them (and not us) your support. Yes, I am asking you not to send us a check, but to place your orders and your donations through that source. That will best strengthen our support network.

We urge you to make use of our publications, listed below. We've sent these to your Senators and Congressman, but they're getting another copy from you, their constituent, is far more persuasive (by the way, neither Captain Evans nor Richard Delgaudio get paid "per book sold").

Publications Available

Peril in Panama, by Richard A. Delgaudio, $6.95 suggested donation.

Death Knell of the Panama Canal? by Captain G. Russell Evans (USCG, Ret.), $4.95 suggested donation.

Big Trouble in Panama, Senate Foreign Relations Committee Testimony of Admiral Thomas Moorer (USN, Ret.), $2 (free with book order)

Red Flag Over the Panama Canal, A Report on the 1998 Mission to Panama, by Richard A. Delgaudio, $2 (free with book order)

Please add postage & handling to all orders: $2 for 1, $4 for up to 10, $10 for up to 50, $15 for 100 or more. Discount on suggested donation: 10% off on 5 or more, 20% off on 10 or more, 30% off on 50 or more, 40% off on 100 or more (a box).

Please address inquiries, orders and/or send donations to:
Richard A. Delgaudio, President ● National Security Center
P.O. Box 96571 ● Washington, DC 20090-65